WHEN
ECONOMICS
MEANS
BUSINESS

WHEN ECONOMICS MEANS BUSINESS

The new economics of
the information age

＊

SULTAN KERMALLY

FINANCIAL TIMES
PITMAN PUBLISHING

FINANCIAL TIMES
MANAGEMENT

LONDON · SAN FRANCISCO
KUALA LUMPUR · JOHANNESBURG

*Financial Times Management delivers the knowledge,
skills and understanding that enable students,
managers and organizations to achieve their ambitions,
whatever their needs, wherever they are.*

London Office:
128 Long Acre, London WC2E 9AN
Tel: +44 (0)171 447 2000
Fax: +44 (0)171 240 5771
Website: www.ftmanagement.com

A Division of Financial Times Professional Limited

First published in Great Britain 1999

© Sultan Kermally 1999

The right of Sultan Kermally to be identified as Author
of this Work has been asserted by him in accordance
with the Copyright, Designs, and Patents Act 1988.

ISBN 0 273 63740 1

British Library Cataloguing in Publication Data
A CIP catalogue record for this book can be obtained
from the British Library.

1 3 5 7 9 10 8 6 4 2

Typeset by M Rules
Printed and bound in Great Britain by
Biddles Ltd, Guildford & King's Lynn

*The Publishers' policy is to use paper manufactured
from sustainable forests.*

ABOUT THE AUTHOR

Sultan Kermally M.A., B.Sc.(Soc.), LL.B., Ph.D., Dip. Fin. & Accts., Dip. Marketing is a management development consultant and trainer designing and delivering training courses in Business Strategy, Business Economics, Marketing, Managing People, Performance and Knowledge, and Personal Development. He has conducted training course in the UK, the Netherlands, Belgium, France, Austria, the Middle East, Hong Kong and Tajikistan.

For several years he held senior academic positions in Scotland and thereafter senior management positions with Management Centre Europe in Brussels, the London Business School and the Economist Intelligence Unit where he held the position of Senior Vice President of the Economist Conferences, Europe.

He has been involved in management education and development for a number of years including distance learning management education courses. He has been tutoring with the Open University and Open University Business School since their inception. Currently he is teaching the 'Performance Management and Evaluation' MBA module for the Open University Business School and the 'Organisational Behaviour' MBA module for the Durham University Business School.

He is the author of *Total Management Thinking*, *Management Ideas* and *Managing Performance*, all published by Butterworth-Heinemann in association with the Institute of Management.

For consultancy and training assignments he can be contacted at 57, Southlands Road, Bromley, Kent, BR2 9QR. Tel: +44 (0) 181 313 3378; Fax: +44 (0) 181 460 1536; e-mail: Skermally@aol.com

This book is dedicated to
my wife and children and to
the Kermally family.

CONTENTS

Gateway Six
NEW PERSPECTIVES ON THE FACTORS
OF PRODUCTION I
Competence and customers

Gateway Seven
NEW PERSPECTIVES ON THE FACTORS
OF PRODUCTION II
Knowledge

ACKNOWLEDGEMENTS

The theme of this book was inspired by Professor W. Brian Arthur of Santa Fe University, Mexico, and Professor John Kay of Oxford University Management School and the enthusiasm of Richard Stagg, publisher of Financial Times Management. Richard demonstrated his enthusiasm for the book by presenting his comments on my submission and by supplying me with various articles, thus sustaining my provocative mode.

One of the features of this book is the use made of different articles appearing in different publications. My thanks go to the following organizations and individuals for their support and permission to reproduce excerpts:

Booz Allen & Hamilton; Customer Service Management, UK; Elsevier Science, Oxford; European Quality Publications Ltd, UK; Financial Times Publications, UK; Foreign Affairs, USA; Harvard Business School Publishing; International Institute For Management Development (IMD), Lausanne, Switzerland; Massachusetts Institute of Technology, Sloan School of Management; McKinsey & Company, UK; Prentice-Hall, USA; Time Inc., USA.

Sincere thanks also go to the following individuals for their support in this venture:

Partha Bose, Editor of *The McKinsey Quarterly*; Mark Feige, Senior Economist, The Economist Intelligence Unit; David Hart and his team, Financial Times Management; Professor John Kay; John Maclean, Marketing Manager, Octel Communications, Europe; V Dharmarajan, Bell Pottinger Communications, London; Professor Jagdish Sheth, Institute for Communications Research & Education, USA; Mr Mirza Pardhan, Director of Education, His Highness the AgaKhan Education Services, France; Tom Peters, a well-known management 'guru' and author; Jean-Pierre Salzman, Director of Public Affairs, IMD, Lausanne; Richard Stagg and staff at Financial Times Management including Linda Dhondy and Phebe Kynaston.

Finally my thanks and love go to my wife Laura for investing an aspect of her life in this book, and to my children Peter, Jenny and Susan and her husband Thomas Powell for their constant encouragement.

Sultan Kermally

INTRODUCTION

Every journey begins with one simple step.

Anon.

Has the time come to reconnect economics with the realities of the modern business world?

Over the centuries the developed world has experienced three distinct ages – the agrarian age, the industrial age and now the information age. This information age is characterized by globalization, rapid technological change, and the importance of knowledge in gaining and sustaining competitive advantage.

The information age has brought into question the appropriateness and usefulness of many concepts and principles embodied in conventional economics. Many management experts and some economists have been seriously considering how to make economics (mainly microeconomics) more intelligible to business executives and to those interested in economics. It seems the two forces of the information age – globalization and technology – do require the rewriting of the basic rules of microeconomics.

This book, the first of its kind on any shelf, makes a down-to-earth attempt to confront the basic principles and concepts of microeconomics with the realities of the information age and to fuse economics with business realities so that it is of practical use in today's business world. Economists like John Kay have raised fundamental questions concerning the pragmatism of economics. Professor Brian Arthur of Santa Fe has been emphasising the dominance of increasing returns in relation to economics in the age of knowledge. Professor Danny Quah of the London School of Economics has put forward the concept of 'the weightless world' to reflect the growing share of the intangible value in economic output. Tom Peters, one of the distinguished management 'gurus', has consistently emphasized the importance of knowledge as a source of the wealth of nations within the context of the new age. This book goes much further by scrutinizing various concepts and principles in microeconomics and examining them within the context of the changes taking place in the business world. New propositions and principles are presented to make sense of economics in practice and make it more meaningful to business in the information age.

How has the information age transformed conventional economics?

The following are but a few examples of how globalization and technological developments have impacted different areas of micro-economics.

- The relevance of diminishing returns has decreased greatly and instead the advent of high tech has bestowed upon 'increasing returns' the respect it deserves.
- In many situations the clear demarcation line between demand and supply as presented in conventional economics has disappeared.
- The marketplace is being transformed into marketspace.
- Global sourcing is dramatically affecting the production possibility frontier in conventional economics.
- The battle between Microsoft and the Department of Justice in the US has brought into prominence the concept of market 'lock-in' in economics.
- Information technology, and in particular the internet, is dramatically affecting price mechanism. Information on prices, quality and availability of goods and services is becoming increasingly available on a global scale, thus making markets more transparent.

- The traditional theory of the firm based on the assumption of profit maximization is being brought into question. The complexity of the business environment is transforming firms into complex adaptive systems.
- The traditional factors of production – land, labour, capital and enterprise – have been transformed into new factors of production – core competencies, customers and knowledge.
- The theory of comparative advantage based on the relative prices of the factors of production underpins the international trade economics. The concept of comparative advantage has been overtaken by the concept of competitive advantage based on the effective use of the new factors of production.

Is all this simply hype?

Many economists believe this is all business hype. Changes are being magnified and exaggerated to discredit conventional economics. This is not so. This book highlights current opinions, research and behaviour of companies like Microsoft, Dell Computers, Hewlett-Packard, Rover, ABB, British Airways, Orange and 3M to support the proposition that *there is a desperate need to review and examine the concepts and principles of conventional economics in order to make them more appropriate to the information age and more meaningful to business executives. There is no advantage in following principles which no longer apply to the 'real world'.*

The rules of economic engagement are undergoing radical change and this impacts the competitive strategies of many businesses. The old laws of production, distribution and consumption are evolving into an integrated theory of demand and supply underpinned by competencies, customers and knowledge as value creating factors of production. Business executives have to understand the new forces underpinning and transforming conventional economics.

Format of the book

This book is practical in approach and is intended for business executives, consultants, economists and students of business and economics. Seven key areas, or 'gateways', are chosen to fuse economics with business within the context of the information age. Each gateway looks at key concepts and principles and puts them under the microscope to examine the changes brought about by globalization and technological development.

- 'Gateway One: Economics at the crossroads – get ready to rip up your economics textbook!' examines the subject matter of economics, the law of diminishing returns, the principle of increasing returns, the production possibility frontier and the division of labour.
- 'Gateway Two: Demand and supply – let's get real' looks at demand, elasticity of demand, supply and price mechanism.
- 'Gateway Three: Competition and markets – from strategy to action' discusses the nature of competition in conventional economics and in reality, the forces of deregulation and what some companies are doing to manage competition.
- 'Gateway Four: Strategic alliances and partnerships – till death do us part!' introduces the subject of strategic alliances and mergers and acquisitions; examines the merger mania of the 1990s, the pros and cons of alliances and mergers, and the actions of trust busters.
- 'Gateway Five: Business organization – making it focused, fast and flexible' questions the basis of the theory of the firm and presents the view that business organizations today have to base their strategies on different and complex factors compared to the strategy of the conventional theory of the firm which is to maximize profits. Cases of Unilever and AT&T are cited.
- 'Gateway Six: New perspectives on the factors of production I – competence and customers' discards the conventional factors of

production – land, labour, capital and enterprise – and presents core competence and customers as new factors of production. Core competence is defined and guidance is given on how to identify it in order to gain competitive advantage. Customers are playing a key role in transforming strategies of organizations such as ABB, DHL, British Airways, TNT and Orange.

● 'Gateway Seven: New perspectives on the factors of production II – knowledge' presents knowledge as the last factor of production. Knowledge is an appreciating asset and underpins the success of organizations in the information age.

Witnesses and verdict

The book makes use of written materials from journals and publications and presents them as 'witnesses' to reinforce and highlight the points made. Such an approach also brings the following advantages:

● it shortens the learning curve of readers;
● it makes readers aware of the range of publications available;
● it provides support to the main theme of the book;
● it exposes the existence of various opinions.

Verdicts appear after the examination of each concept and principle to consolidate the conclusion of the evidence. This method of presentation brings about variety in style and creates a user-friendly approach.

Gateway One

ECONOMICS AT THE CROSSROADS

Get ready to rip up your economics textbook!

I would like to see economics become more of a science, and more of a science means that it concerns itself more with reality . . . We're facing a danger that economics is rigorous deduction based upon faulty assumptions.

Professor W. Brian Arthur, Santa Fe Institute

INTRODUCTION

In the past few decades the business world has witnessed many changes which have affected the competitive positioning of countries. Some countries such as Singapore, Malaysia and Taiwan, which not long ago were classified as 'underdeveloped', have risen to become 'economic tigers'. What have been the main drivers which have transformed such countries and the international business world in general? What has been the implication of the changing political ideologies of many countries? What effect do such changes have on the fundamental principles of economics such as diminishing returns and the division of labour? In a situation like this, how can we get economics to make sense in the world in which we live?

THE CHANGING NATURE OF THE BUSINESS PROFILE

In recent years there have been wide-ranging discussions covering the problems facing Asian tigers, the effect of Economic Monetary Union (EMU) on businesses, and the changing fortunes of the Japanese economy and its effect on other economies. Gloomy forecasts from various experts show how Asia's financial crisis is squeezing the global economy.

At the beginning of 1998 the Economist Intelligence Unit forecast showed how the former communist countries will replace the tiger economies of South East Asia as the world's hot-spots. These are the changes taking place at macro and geo-political level.

At microeconomic level mergers and acquisitions activity is increasing. Strategic alliances and mergers are affecting telecommunications, pharmaceutical and retail sectors throughout the world. Organizations are abandoning their rigid structures and converting them into flat and flexible structures. The processes of production are being re-engineered and employees are being empowered. The world of economics at macro and micro levels is turning topsy-turvy as a result of the process of globalization. Economic decisions and changes in the economic environment have been fundamental drivers of business strategy. It is therefore important to understand to what extent the subject matter and the principles and models underpinning economics are being affected by the globalization of business.

Enter the 'global economy'

What is this force that has prompted many authors to write doomsday books on the subject of 'The Death of Distance', 'The Death of the Banker', 'The Death of Money' and even 'The Death of Economics'?

> *The world of economics at macro and micro levels is turning topsy-turvy as a result of the process of globalization.*

Since 1980 organizations have viewed the world market as a triad comprising the regions of Asia–Pacific, the North Americas and Europe. This view has come about because of intensive competition. Being a global company does not mean the same as being a multi-national company (MNC). Traditionally, multi-national companies sell to a number of countries, adjusting product offerings, manufacturing practices and marketing strategies. They operate in the overseas markets often through their subsidiaries taking strategies and 'command' from national headquarters.

According to Theodore Levitt of Harvard Business School, the global corporation knows everything about one great thing. It knows about the absolute need to be competitive on a worldwide basis as well as nationally and seeks constantly to drive down prices by standardizing what it sells and how it operates. It treats the world as if it were composed of a few standardized markets rather than many customized markets. It works toward global convergence.

Business International, a company once owned by the Economist Newspaper, listed in 1991 the following main attributes of 'the global company':

- more products are sold outside the home territory than within it;
- decision making is localized not centralized;
- R&D is implemented whenever necessary – often in foreign laboratories;
- company stock is usually listed on several foreign exchanges;
- shareholders are spread around the world;
- national executives are on the fast track to top management;
- significant numbers of non-national directors are on the board;
- trade barriers are not a threat to business;
- multiple identities and loyalties are successfully managed, in part through a fluid chain of command;
- its global image is bolstered, rather than confined, by strong home country identity.

A company needs to assume international perspectives in its various operations in order to become a truly global company.

The formation of 'borderless organizations'

Changing political ideologies and a climate of collaboration have facilitated 'borderless organizations'. Texas Instruments' high speed telecommunications chip was conceived by engineers from Ericsson Telephone Co. in Sweden and designed in Nice with software tools the company had developed in Houston. Electrolux has a research laboratory in Finland, a development centre in Sweden and a design group in Italy. Skills and knowledge are now being managed across borders.

These are but a few examples of forces of globalization creating 'borderless organizations'. Global competition, the changing mindset of international business executives, indeed the changing profile of whole international businesses are contributing to a renaissance in the way the subject of economics should be approached.

Globalization has not impacted all countries equally. Many countries in sub-Saharan Africa are the least globalized. There are many reason for this imbalance but the two main reasons are macroeconomic instability and regional trade barriers. However, sooner rather than later these countries will have to organize themselves in order to reap the economies of globalization.

So far nothing much in economics, and in particular, microeconomics has changed. Why? Peter Drucker (1986), the doyen of management gurus, wrote:

> It may be a long time before economic theorists accept that there have been fundamental changes, and longer still before they adapt their theories to account for them. Above all, they will surely be most reluctant to accept that it is the world economy in control, rather than macroeconomics of the nation-state on which most economic theory still exclusively focuses."
>
> Source: Peter Drucker, 'The changed world economy', Foreign Affairs, Vol. 64 No. 4, 1986, pp. 768–91. Reprinted by permission of Foreign Affairs. Copyright 1986 by the Council of Foreign Relations, Inc.

Is globalization here to stay?

The diffusion of innovation and convergence of technologies will play a key role in accelerating the globalization process and will make the 'global village' a reality. Globalization will also affect the way we do transactions with one another. According to William W. Lewis and Marvin Harris of McKinsey & Co. (1992):

> Our view is that a virtuous, upward-ratcheting cycle of economic convergence and technology transfer, driven in a large measure by the actions of transitional corporations and the expectations of well-informed

consumers, will drive globalization forward – despite all obstacles in its path. These corporations are transforming the way wealth itself is created, deriving ever greater productivity from the wide and rapid diffusion of improved know-how or innovation.

. . . globalization – the spread of economic innovation around the world and the political and cultural adjustments that accompany this diffusion – cannot be stopped. This is because it is not the result of a fitful lunge by government or military power toward ever larger geopolitical entities. Nor is it the product of some growing ideological conformity on how we should live. It is, rather, the organic result of the virtuous cycle described above, by which economic convergence and the diffusion of innovation raise standards of living over time. As history teaches, the political organizations and ideologies that yield superior economic performance survive, flourish, and replace those that are less productive.

Source: Reprinted with permission of the publisher from William W. Lewis and Marvin Harris, 'Why globalization must prevail'. *The McKinsey Quarterly*, No. 2, 1992, pp. 115. Copyright 1992 McKinsey & Company. All rights reserved.

Economics studies how society makes decisions in relation to the use of resources which are scarce and which have alternative uses. The decisions relate to what goods and services should be produced, how they should be produced and for whom.

Whether businesses operate in a democratic society or not, decisions relating to the allocation and use of scarce resources have to be made. Resources such as land, labour, capital and raw materials are scarce relative to the demand for these resources. The concept of relative scarcity is fundamental in economics. In addition, these scarce resources have alternative uses. Land can be used for farming, building roads, building houses and so on. Every resource in a society has alternative uses. If land is used to build a motorway instead of being converted into a country park, then the motorway has been built at

> *The diffusion of innovation and convergence of technologies will play a key role in accelerating the globalization process.*

the expense of a country park. The other concept in economics is that of *opportunity cost*. The opportunity cost of a motorway, in our example, is a country park. The opportunity cost is a sacrificed alternative.

Many business executives do not reflect upon the nature of economics because they do not relate their own decision making to the decisions of governments that represent societies. In other words, business executives do not see how their actions affect decisions made at macro level.

In businesses, whether small or big, decisions have to be made to determine the nature of the business. What business are we in and where do we want to go are two fundamental questions driving the formulation of corporate strategy. Once business strategy is formulated, decisions have to be made as to what, for whom and how to produce. Such decisions relate to the amount and type of technology to be used, what type of people to employ, what competencies are needed to succeed in the business, where to sell and for how much. These are all decisions that mirror those that have to be made by governments at macro level.

Decisions made in the business environment are the macrocosm of decisions made in society in relation to the use of resources to produce goods and services. Economics, therefore, relates to human behaviour as a relationship between ends and means which have alternative uses. Those who have to make decisions at macro and micro level have to make sure that the scarce resources are used efficiently and effectively.

Efficiency is doing the right thing whereas effectiveness is doing the right thing right. Effectiveness in economics would mean using scarce resources to achieve objectives set at micro and macro level.

To what extent has globalization affected the nature of economics? The fundamental proposition of economics as a subject which relates to the allocation of scarce resources has not been affected. What has been transformed is the concept of *relative scarcity* which has been broadened in its scope as a result of the availability and use of resources worldwide.

ECONOMIC CONCEPTS AND MODELS – QUESTIONING FOUR TENETS OF ECONOMICS

The following four tenets of economics will be questioned:

- the law of diminishing returns
- increasing returns
- the production possibility frontier
- the division of labour.

1 The law of diminishing returns

The concepts of *relative scarcity* and the *opportunity cost* will remain fundamental concepts in spite of globalization. However, what has changed and is changing is the scope of these concepts. Resources are scarce in relation to the demand for goods and services not only locally or nationally, but also globally.

Everyone who has studied economics has come across the law of diminishing returns. According to this law, if we increase the use of any one factor, for example labour, assuming all other factors (such as machinery, technology, raw materials) remain constant then every additional worker will contribute less to the total output than the previous person. Even though the total output increases, the additional output, known as marginal output, will fall (*see* Fig. 1.1).

This happens because we assume that resources, apart from the number of workers in our example, are fixed. In addition, we assume technical production conditions are given and constant. Within the context of these assumptions the law of diminishing returns will come into existence. According to the economists this phenomenon occurs as long as one of the factors of production is fixed.

Number of workers	Total output (units)	Average output (units)	Marginal output (units)
10	1000	100	—
11	1760	160	—
12	2160	180	200
13	2350	180.77	190
14	2500	178.57	150
15	2600	173.30	100

Fig. 1.1 The law of diminishing returns

Let us take a business where we are using resources A, B, C and D to produce goods. We assume that resources B, C, and D are at present not being used to full capacity. If we then increase resource A, the additional unit will make a higher contribution (return) to output. Once one of resources B, C, and D reaches its full capacity and its supply remains constant, further additions of A will make a diminishing contribution to output. The law of diminishing returns will set in.

This 'law' was formulated by Reverend Thomas Malthus in 1798. Malthus predicted poverty and the demise of many businesses on the basis of the law of diminishing returns. More than anyone else, it was Malthus who was responsible for earning political economy the name of the 'dismal science'.

Two hundred years on we are still faced with this 'law' in economics. Economists tell us that the resources in the world are not finite and as long as one of the factors of production becomes scarce the nation and businesses will face the law of diminishing returns. Economists believe that highlighting this 'law' constitutes a continuing challenge to come up with new and better solutions to use scarce resources efficiently.

This can be regarded as a defensive and weak statement. Technological developments have taken place not because scientists and technocrats have been challenged by the existence of the law of diminishing returns, but because they have responded to the changing business, customer needs and climate on a global scale.

The role of global sourcing

The conventional wisdom in economics is that manufacturers and retailers procure materials from domestic suppliers. This helps to maintain predictable deliveries and keep costs down and ensure control over supplier quality. This conventional wisdom has now been turned upside down as businesses have been globalized.

Philip Kotler (1994), marketing guru, writes:

> The world economy has undergone a radical transformation in the last two decades. Basically, geographical and cultural distances have shrunk significantly with the advent of jet airlines, fax machines, global computer and telephone linkups, and world television satellite broadcasting. This shrinkage of distance has permitted companies to widen substantially their geographical markets as well as their supplier sources. In the past, a US company such as Chrysler would build its cars from components mostly sourced in the United States and would sell most of its cars in the US marketplace. Today, Chrysler orders its components from suppliers in Japan, Korea, Germany, and a dozen other countries and also sells its cars in other parts of the world. One is no longer sure that Chrysler-labelled cars were primarily made by Chrysler.
>
> Companies in various industries are also developing their products using a global assembly line. Consider the following:
>
> In the past, most American clothing was made and sold in America. Much cutting and sewing were done in New York and New England 'sweatshops' by immigrant labour working long hours. The workers joined the unions and raised wages. Searching for lower labour costs, many clothing manufacturers moved to Southern states. More recently many US companies moved their manufacturing to Asia. Today, Bill Blass, one of America's top fashion designers, will examine woven cloth made from Australian wool with printed design prepared in Italy. He will design a dress and fax the drawing to his Hong Kong agent who will place the order with a mainland China factory. The finished dresses will be

airfreighted to New York where they will be redistributed to departmental stores that had placed orders . . .

Is the Boeing 767 an American plane? Boeing's staff in Seattle designed the plane and manufactured the wings and cockpit. The nose tip and certain wing parts were manufactured in Italy, the rear section in Canada, the front windshields and engines in England, and the fuselage and high-tech components in Japan. Altogether 29 countries participated in producing this plane.

Source: Philip Kotler, *Marketing Management* (1994) 8th edn, pp. 12–13. Reprinted by permission of Prentice-Hall, Inc., USA. Copyright 1994.

Kotler, writing from a marketing perspective, is reinforcing the point made by Lewis and Harris that the convergence of technologies is shrinking distances and it is important now to view products and markets as being global. Increasingly the expectations of consumers are being globalized as well.

In 1986, a survey of 80 large US firms was conducted by the Machinery and Allied Products Institute. The survey found that the amount spent on offshore purchases grew from 11 per cent in the early 1980s to more than 15 per cent in 1986. The trend is also increasing in the case of European manufacturers.

> *A key benefit of global sourcing is the ability to achieve significant cost savings while maintaining or improving quality and service.*

A key benefit of global sourcing is the ability to achieve significant cost savings while maintaining or improving quality and service. In the case of China, for example, A. T. Kearney, one of the leading management consultancy firms, has found that an efficient global sourcing effort contributes an extra $150 million to the bottom line for every $1 billion. Costs are not the only consideration. Low-skilled labour costs are a falling share of total production costs in most globally competitive manufacturing industries. Labour costs now represent only 5–10 per cent (1990) as opposed to 25 per cent in the 1970s, according to the Organisation for Economic Co-operation and Development. Other considerations are availability of materials, quality, and speed of delivery.

In the 1990s many manufacturers from West European countries are choosing Central and Eastern European suppliers as a source of materials in order to control costs and because of the region's proximity to Europe. These suppliers in the region are very keen to make sourcing contracts as a result of privatization policy in their region. The state can no longer be relied upon to provide employment.

Manufacturers nowadays have international markets to source for raw materials, labour, capital and so on. The resources, therefore, are scarce relative to demand in the home market, but because they are used and sourced globally, this is no longer a significant factor.

However, some economists still hang on to the law of diminishing returns to explain some modern economic phenomena such as a crisis in the East Asian economies. In the Survey of East Asian Economies which appeared in *The Economist* of 7 March 1998, it was stated that some experts believed some time ago that East Asia will experience a slowdown in its economic achievements. Economists like Paul Krugman always argued that there was never an East Asian economic miracle. What has been achieved has been the result of perspiration rather than inspiration. Diminishing returns will set in once all labour and capital are fully utilized.

The law of diminishing returns is also alive in the economies of countries like Tajikistan. According to the Economist Intelligence Unit's report on Tajikistan, the origins of GDP in 1995 were: agriculture and forestry 40.3 per cent, industry 15.5 per cent and construction 6.6 per cent. The economy is dominated by primary sectors where, without accelerated technological development, diminishing returns will set in and reduce the productivity and subsequently growth in Tajikistan.

The law of diminishing returns in advanced economies

Over the past few decades socio-economic and technological developments have made the assumptions behind the law of diminishing returns almost redundant. If we examine the practice of global sourcing and global production alone, we are prompted to ask the question: 'Why is the law of diminishing returns still presented in economics packaged in its old assumptions?' Professor W. Brian Arthur of Santa Fe Institute argues that in a high-tech economy the focus of attention should shift from diminishing returns to increasing returns. This view will be examined in detail later.

VERDICT

The time has not yet come to bury completely the law of diminishing returns. In the 1990s we do have many small and medium size enterprises (SMEs), which are very slow in responding to the globalization process. For them this law will impact their business and their cost of production unless they start thinking globally. However, diminishing returns as a key principle has to take back seat in the information age economy.

---

2 From diminishing returns to increasing returns

Increasing returns as a concept is explained in economics within the context of returns to scale (size) – that is, the effect of scale increases the impact of inputs on the quantity produced. The returns to scale reflect the responsiveness of the total product when *all* the inputs are increased proportionately.

When production is undertaken it is difficult to divide all the factors in exactly the proportion required. As a result, fixed costs are spread over all units of output as output is increased. This means the average cost per unit of output falls at the early stages of production.

Eventually, as production increases, economies of scale are wiped out and decreasing returns to scale set in.

Increasing returns to scale underpin the downward sloping average cost and total cost curves of a firm as we will examine later on. According to Paul Samuelson, economies of scale and mass production have fuelled much of the economic growth of nations over the last century. Most production processes are many times larger than they were during the nineteenth century.

Some economists are now focusing attention on the concept of increasing returns as such rather than increasing returns to scale in order to explain some business phenomena. The following is a piece written by James Aley (1996):

THE THEORY THAT MADE MICROSOFT

It's called 'increasing returns' and it's one of the hottest and most important ideas in economics today.

Anyone who's taken freshman economics knows how economists cherish the concept of diminishing returns. It's one of those theoretical pillars that keeps the dismal science dismal. The more you make or sell, the harder it gets. If there are profits to be had in, say the dog food business, you won't be the only one fighting for the spoils, and whatever spoils there are to start with won't last long.

But there's a problem with the diminishing returns version of the world. Sometimes, markets do just the opposite of what diminishing returns says they should, and all the rewards gravitate toward one winner at the expense of everyone else – and sometimes that winner doesn't even have the best product. How did we end up with the awkward QWERTY configuration on our typewriters and computer keyboards? Why did VHS become the standard for videocassette recorders, when Betamax was the better technology?

In other words, in some cases, the more someone makes or sells something, the *easier* it gets. Obviously something other than diminishing returns is going on in the economy – namely, *increasing returns*. This insight can explain many otherwise puzzling phenomena in the modern world, and a growing school of thought has formed around increasing returns. The idea may become as central a tenet of modern economics as supply and demand, and is already well on its way to achieving buzz word status. Microsoft's Bill Gates, for instance – never far from the cutting edge – devotes a good chunk of his recent book, *The Road Ahead*, to increasing returns, although he refers to the idea as 'positive feedback'.

According to one of the foremost theorists of this new school, W. Brian Arthur, an economist at both Stanford and the Santa Fe Institute, increasing returns is essentially the tendency for something that gets ahead to get further ahead. 'The more people use your product', he says, 'the more advantage you have – or, to put it in another way, the bigger your installed base, the better off you are.'

The QWERTY keyboard, named for the first six letters in the upper row, is a simple example Arthur uses to illustrate this principle. QWERTY didn't become standard because it was more efficient than other possible layouts. In fact, the configuration was designed to slow typists down, because early typewriters kept jamming. The historical event that made this inefficient layout ubiquitous was Remington Sewing Machine Co's decision to manufacture its typewriters using QWERTY. Remington made a lot of typewriters and the configuration eventually achieved 'lock-in'. The more Remington typewriters that were on people's desks and the more typists got used to the layout, the less willing users would be to switch to a different one. The larger the population of crack QWERTY typists, the more important it became for aspiring typists to learn to use it. And we've muddled along ever since.

The most extreme examples of the way increasing returns works in the real world today appear in the computer software business, where establishing a big user base is the key to success. It's the reason that Microsoft wins virtually every market share battle it enters, even when its products aren't necessarily the best. Microsoft set a standard for personal computer operating systems that 'locked in' and consequently gave it a huge advantage in selling its spreadsheet and word-processing software.

Other characteristics of the software business, and high tech in general, amplify the effects. First there is the upfront cost of development. High tech products require enormous investment in R&D but once the products are ready to roll, manufacturing costs are relatively low. Microsoft, Arthur says, spent hundreds of millions developing Windows 95, but it costs Microsoft almost nothing to make more copies. And in fact, the more copies the company puts on the shelves, the more it sells, because the more people use Windows 95, the more software gets developed for it. The more software is available, the more people buy Windows 95.

. . . Economists – especially economic theorists – have long known about increasing returns; they just never did anything with the idea. (The great British economist Alfred Marshall, who laid the foundation for much of the modern economics, wrote about the phenomenon in his seminal textbook published in 1890.) It took the advent of high tech and the personal computer for increasing returns to get the respect it deserves.

Mainstream economists shunned the idea of increasing returns for both methodological and ideological reasons. Practically, increasing returns turns out to be exceedingly difficult to deal with mathematically; it muddies the mechanics of supply and demand, which in classical theory meet at a final price that clears the market. Ideologically, increasing returns runs against the general point of departure for orthodox economists; that, other things being equal, market forces automatically yield the best possible outcome – the best product at the best price – and no one runs away with the market because the minute you make a profit, someone else sees an opportunity and enters the fray.

Increasing returns isn't completely mainstream yet – it isn't taught as a part of standard introductory economics courses. But at least the mere mention of the concept no longer causes economists to grimace and inhale sharply. Arthur's work has provided much of the mathematical rigour needed to make the idea legitimate. Significant contributions also come from Stanford's Paul Krugman, and Paul Romer at the University of California at Berkeley – two of the Young Turks among modern macroeconomists. Krugman's work has concentrated on how increasing returns plays out in international trade and challenges another deeply held conviction of economists: that free trade among nations always produces the best economic outcome. Romer has been working the concept into his theories of general economic growth.

. . . the new thinking about increasing returns helps us to understand why the Microsoft's, Mercks, and Intels of the world operate by rules that economists either had long believed impossible or had chosen to ignore.

Businesses like Microsoft are changing the fundamental principles which dominated economics for a very long time. One of these is the principle of diminishing returns. Now some economists are advocating the dominance of increasing returns – the more there is of something, the bigger the advantage in reaping yet more. Microsoft is in that situation. During 1997 alone, Microsoft:

- acquired Hotmail, a free Web e-mail service
- invested $445 million in speech-recognition software maker Lernout & Hauspie
- invested $150 million in Apple, part of a technology swapping deal
- acquired VXtreme which makes software for sending video over the net
- formed a joint venture with First Data for on-line bill paying
- acquired Coopers & Peters which makes Java-based interface software
- acquired WebTV
- acquired Interse which makes web-site analysis software.

Now some economists are advocating the dominance of increasing returns – the more there is of something, the bigger the advantage in reaping yet more.

The business world will be dominated by the likes of Microsoft and increasing returns, which according to economist John Hicks was 'the wreckage of the greater part of economic theory', will be its salvation. According to Professor Quah of the London School of Economics, we are in the world of 'weightless economy' which puts emphasis on the intangible value in economic output. Brian Arthur of Santa Fe Institute tells us that we are dealing now with 'cognitive industry' in which ideas are worth billions, while products themselves cost little. Such a world questions the dominance of diminishing returns in economics.

Brian Arthur of Santa Fe Institute has advocated the dominance of increasing returns in the world of high tech. He says, 'Like or not, we are entering a phase in which the economy is dominated by technology – therefore dominated by increasing returns and by permanent transience, instead of equilibrium.' He comments, 'Science after science is losing its sense of certainty. Maths, physics, biology, all of them. It is the same in the arts, in music. Why should economics be the exception?'

In an interview with Professor W. Brian Arthur (Kurtzman, 1998), Professor Arthur says:

> In high tech, though, there are two or three characteristics that overturn diminishing returns and give you increasing returns, meaning the more advantage you have towards getting ahead, the more advantage you have towards getting further ahead. You can call it positive feedback. No one uses the phrase nowadays of increasing returns to scale – this is not a scale phenomenon. Increasing returns simply means that whoever gets advantage, gets further advantage. Whoever loses advantage – think of Apple Computer – will lose further advantage. Encyclopaedia Britannica, TWA 10 years ago, IBM. You start to lose advantage, you get in a worse position. You gain advantage, you get in a better position.
>
> Why? For three reasons. The first is cost advantage. High tech products – things like Microsoft Windows 95 – are complicated to design and require huge amounts in upfront R&D costs. With Windows 95, that came to $250 million for the first disc. But the second disc just a few cents. So does the third. The more you produce in the lifetime of that product, the lower your per unit cost. In other words, the more cost advantage you have, the larger your market gets.
>
> Secondly, there are what economists call network effects. That means the bigger a network gets, the more I'm likely to need to join that network. For example, as more people use Java, the downloading language

for the Internet, the more likely it is I would have to have Java in my computer to download off the Net. As fewer people use its competitor, ActiveX, it is less likely that I would have to have ActiveX.

Thirdly, there are what I call groove-in effects tied to customers and consumers. Basically, this means that the more I use a product, the more I'm familiar with that product, the more convenient it gets for me. I use Microsoft Word. There might be a better program out there, but I know all the tricks with Word that I mastered over several years and I am very reluctant to give that up to start again with another product.

So these characteristics produce increasing returns. The more Java is out in the market, the more prevalent Java gets in the market, the more advantage it gets.

Source: Joel Kurtzman, 'Thought leader: W Brian Arthur'. *Strategy & Business*, second quarter, pp. 98–9. By permission of Booze Allen & Hamilton.

Some critics of Professor Arthur's view argue that his assertion applies only to the world of technology. In the area of consumer goods manufacturing and service, diminishing returns dominate. Is this view valid?

When one looks at how the whole process of value adding has been transformed (consumers becoming one of the factors of production, acquisition of knowledge and diffusion of knowledge within organizations) it is clear that the concept of increasing returns is gaining prominence.

VERDICT

With the convergence of technologies taking place more dramatically in the telecommunications sector and with the fever of mergers, acquisitions, strategic alliances and partnerships, and with the increase in high-tech industries incorporating cost advantage, network effects and groove-in effects, the focus of attention in business and in economics will shift to the concept of increasing returns. This will be the dominant principle in modern day economics.

3 The production possibility frontier

The production possibility frontier reflects the subject matter of economics which is the allocation of scarce resources. The production possibility diagram expresses the concept of opportunity cost, i.e. the sacrificed alternative involved in economic decision making.

Let us assume that all goods produced by a society are categorized as goods A and all services produced by the same society as goods B. The production possibility frontier diagram shows that at a particular given time the society in question produces X_1 of A and Y_1 of B. The production possibility frontier shows the maximum amount of B that can be produced for each level of output of goods A (*see* Fig. 1.2).

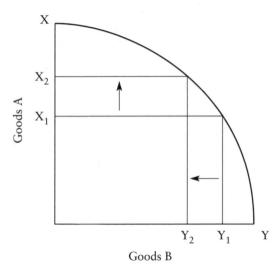

Fig 1.2 The production possibility frontier

Curve XY shows all the combinations of A and B that can be produced at a given time. The shape of the curve XY is based on the law of diminishing returns. If the society decides to produce more of A, say X_2, then it will have to sacrifice production of B and produce Y_2 of B. The opportunity cost of producing X_1–X_2 more of A is Y_1–Y_2 less of B.

Let us take the example of the car manufacturing sector and assume cars are manufactured to meet demand domestically and abroad (export demand). Assuming all resources are deployed at a given time then the manufacturing sector produces OA of cars for the home market and OB for the export market. If it wants to export more cars, say to OB_1, then it will have fewer cars, OA_1, for the domestic market (*see* Fig. 1.3).

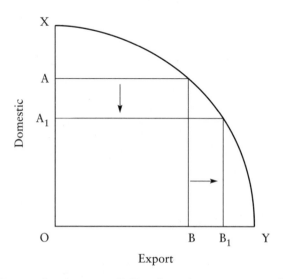

Fig. 1.3 The production possibility frontier – car manufacturing

However, if all resources are not fully employed then it is possible to produce more of one or both goods without any opportunity cost if production is taking place within the production possibility frontier below the curve XY. The sector can produce more of A and more of B and move towards the production possibility frontier. Once it starts producing at any point on curve XY, an increase in production of any one category of goods will be at the expense of producing other categories of goods.

Most economics textbooks use the production possibility frontier to highlight the debate about society's choice between social services and private goods. As Samuelson used to put it, 'The choice is between guns and butter.' The production possibility frontier is a model that can be used to illustrate various arguments in relation to the use of resources by governments to provide education and/or health services or to produce goods for defence. It is also used to illustrate the use of resources by private and public sectors and how such decisions 'crowd out' investment opportunities available to both sectors.

The production possibilities concept and model in economics serve to explain, in a very simple way, the debate on the allocation of resources. The frontier can be shifted to the right by using resources efficiently.

Resources in economics are called 'factors of production' and they are categorized into land, labour, capital and enterprise. These factors of production are key inputs to output and are the source of value creation in economics.

- Land incorporates all natural resources. It represents land for farming, building houses, roads and factories and also all energy resources such as water, gas and electricity.
- Labour consists of human beings engaged in the production process. This factor includes manual and non-manual workers involved in producing goods and services.
- Capital includes machines and other physical assets produced in order to facilitate further production such as tools, transport vehicles, factories and so on.
- Enterprise is the fourth factor which co-ordinates all the other factors of production to facilitate manufacturing goods and providing services.

When we refer to using resources in economics we mean the use of land, labour, capital and enterprise. Generally speaking, relative to all other factors of production, land is relatively scarce. In a short period the supply of land is fixed so entrepreneurs can add labour and capital to produce goods. In a very short period, the law of diminishing returns will set in. Because of the relative scarcity of land the law of diminishing returns has become one of the core concepts in economics. The production possibility frontier is a model reflecting the boundary of production using all factors of production at a given time.

Is the production possibility frontier a valid model?

The production possibility frontier is an effective model to get across the concept of an opportunity cost which underpins the subject matter of economics. But the world economy is changing so fast that it questions the validity of this model except in dealing with a very short period. John Naisbitt and Patricia Aburdene (1990) emphasize the fact that increasingly the world was becoming a single economy. The world economies are all interlinked.

The production possibility frontier model in economics must be presented as a most dynamic model rather than in a static fashion packaged with old assumptions. According to Naisbitt and Aburdene (1990):

> there are no limits to growth. The global boom of the 1990s will be free of the limits on growth we have known in the past. In fact, there will be virtually no limits to growth. There will be an abundance of natural resources throughout the 1990s, from agricultural products and raw materials to oil. Everything that comes out of the ground will be in over supply for the balance of this century and probably much longer.
>
> Since the mid-1980s there has been more than enough food to feed the world's population; hunger persists because of political and distribution problems. Population growth has slowed almost everywhere, except Africa, and in many areas has slowed dramatically. Furthermore, we are poised on the edge of another green revolution through biotechnology.
>
> We need fewer materials, as we have been moving away from material-intensive products for decades – for example, the widespread substitution of plastics to steel. Miniaturisation is another factor lessening demand for

materials. In recent years the prices of raw materials have been the lowest in recorded history in relation to manufactured goods and services. In general, they will continue to fall.

A prototypical example of the shift away from the material-intensive is fibre-optic cable. Just seventy pounds of the fibre-optic cable can transmit as many messages as one ton of copper wire. Equally important, those seventy pounds of fibre-optic cable require less than 5 per cent of the energy needed to produce one ton of copper wire.

In both materials and energy, that is an analogue for the new economy. And before the year 2000 a single optic fibre will be able to transmit 10 million conversations at the same time, compared with 3000 in 1988.

With such happenings how can a static production possibility frontier make any sense?

VERDICT

The production possibility frontier is an interesting model. In practice it is extremely dynamic due to socio-political and economic-technological changes. It can only be used to convey the notion of an opportunity cost when making a very short-term economic and business analysis based on static assumptions. It also serves as a benchmark for using resources at macro and micro level efficiently, as in the very short term resources at macro and micro level are finite. Apart from such use it makes no sense in a modern context.

---

4 The division of labour

When examining the concept of the production possibility frontier, one of the ways of improving efficiency in the use of resources so that production can be placed at the frontier, or the production possibility frontier can be shifted to the right, was specialization of resources – the division of labour.

In 1776, Adam Smith, one of the great economists, wrote a book entitled *An Inquiry into the Natures and Causes of the Wealth of Nations*. In chapter one Smith wrote '. . . the greatest improvement in the production powers of labour, and the greater part of the skill, dexterity, and judgement with which it is anywhere directed, or applied, seem to have been the effects of the division of labour.'

He emphasized the importance of the division of labour by giving what has now become a famous example, that of a pin factory. Smith visited a pin factory and observed that when one man specialized in putting heads on the pins, another in sharpening the points, another in placing them on cards and so forth, together they could produce 100 times more than could the same number of men working separately to perform all functions.

Smith explained that, if each worker concentrated on a small operation in the manufacture of an article, instead of performing every operation in its construction, production would be greatly increased, and greater efficiency obtained. He attributed these results to three facts:

- to the increase of dexterity in every particular workman
- to the saving of time which is commonly lost in passing from one species of work to another
- to the invention of a great many machines which facilitate labour, and enable one man to do the work of many.

The division of labour is specialization on the part of the labour force. Specialization occurs when production is divided into a number of small specialized steps or tasks and each person or group of persons performs a specialized task.

The division of labour and its influence on business

The principle of the division of labour had significant influence on organizational structures. Businesses began to be organized on the basis of functional specialization. Many management pioneers, like

Frederick Taylor, Lilian and Frank Gilbreth and Henri Fayol to name but a few, focused attention on management structure, operations and functions. A typical business structure evolved and looked like the structure shown in Fig. 1.4.

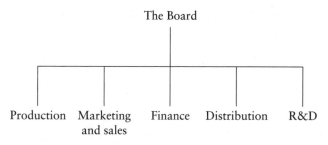

Fig 1.4 A typical business structure

All key functions of business were compartmentalized and people working in each compartment specialized in different skills such as production, engineering, finance and sales. Thus the division of labour underpinned the structure of organizations.

Early in the twentieth century the two automobile pioneers, Henry Ford and Alfred Sloan, adopted the principle of division of labour in their plants. Ford broke down car assembling into a series of uncomplicated tasks. Instead of each worker walking from one assembly to the next performing simple repetitive tasks, Ford invented the moving assembly line which brought the work to the worker.

Prior to the assembly line, automobiles were manufactured by groups of workers who jointly shared all aspects of the assembly job. Under Ford's plan, workers were each assigned a specific task (mounting tyres on wheels, tightening lug nuts and so on) on the line. The result was an increase in productivity and a reduction in unit cost. The division of labour also reduced the need for highly skilled labour; it led to the de-skilling of labour.

Ford made constant improvements in the production process and it became more integrated and mechanized. The strategy of cost minimization involved centralization and backward and forward integration to reap economies of scale. However, as the market began to change, Ford found it increasingly difficult to vary its product and change its cost structure which led to subsequent difficulties.

Alfred Sloan extended the division of labour to the management system. He established the division of professional labour, an extension of the division of manual labour that took place at factory floor. He introduced the concept of 'decentralization with co-ordinated control'.

Sloan, in his book *The Management: How it works*, emphasized the importance of specialization and the division of labour. If the supplying divisions within the company, as a result of adopting division of labour, could not offer lower cost and as a result lower prices then the purchasing division within the company would be free to buy from outside sources. It was Sloan who advocated a notion of what we now call outsourcing and global sourcing.

Henry Ford's and Arthur Sloan's ideas of management underpinned by the concept of division of labour put forward by Adam Smith lasted for a number of decades. Their ideas were geared towards achieving efficiency and the result was pushing the production possibility frontier outwards.

VERDICT

The concept of the division of labour is still valid today in business and in society. Specialization, an extension of the division of labour, provides core competencies to conduct business in a global environment. However, what is important to understand is that specialization should not be practised to its extreme as Sloan advocated and practised in his assembly line factories. The focus of attention nowadays is on lean and agile organizations which require specialists to work together in teams (multi-functional teams).

MODERN BUSINESS INITIATIVES AND THEIR IMPACT ON THE KEY ECONOMIC CONCEPTS AND MODELS

The following selected initiatives will be examined to highlight and reinforce how business is diverging from some of the established economic principles and thinking:

- the introduction of cross-functional teams
- the horizontal organization – the death of hierarchies
- re-engineering processes to use resources effectively and get close to customers.

This divergence impacts economic thinking and analysis.

However, over the last two decades the production possibility frontiers have been attacked by various forces and initiatives in order for businesses to compete globally. It is important for economics to take these initiatives on board and to examine their effect on business at micro and macro level. The focus of attention at micro and macro level has shifted to producing goods and services that would compete effectively in the global competitive arena by adopting total quality management systems, paying attention and getting close to customers, redesigning organizational structure by questioning conventional wisdom based on the division of labour, developing workers' core competencies and delivering service excellence.

Specialization versus cross-functional teams

From the world of specialization we move to the world of teams and especially cross-functional teams. Cross-functional teams consist of members who represent different skill sets and competencies. Different specialists are grouped together in small teams to perform special tasks and functions. Working in cross-functional teams brings about cross-fertilization of different functions which add value to the outcome. Such teams generate synergy and it is claimed that they lead to cost savings, innovation and customer satisfaction.

> *Working in cross-functional teams brings about cross-fertilization of different functions which add value to the outcome.*

Rover Group used cross-functional teams to launch the Land Rover Discovery. Such team work saved two years of the usual product development cycle time. Global competition has necessitated employees taking on fewer and more flexible roles. As one managing director in the electronics industry put it, 'If we start working more cross-functionally then we should not think of our people as locked in their little boxes on the organizational chart. Instead we should think of our people as resources on call.'

Organizations like Federal Express, Motorola, AT&T, Boeing and the like have boosted productivity and improved the quality of their products and services by organizing their workforces in teams. Even in countries like India, in some high tech companies traditional working methods are replaced by cross-functional teams. It is reported that Fiat opened a plant in southern Italy and spent $64 million training workers to operate in independent teams.

When Adam Smith put forward his theory of the division of labour he advocated each individual specializing in one specific task of the production process rather than an individual performing multiple tasks. This way output per person will be very high. Nowadays we are told team work enhances the quality of the product and the quality of decision making in business. Teams outperform the same set of individuals operating in a non-team mode, particularly where multiple skills, experiences and judgements determine performance.

Labour, as it has been considered in traditional economics, no longer constitutes a factor of production. On this basis the division of labour becomes obsolete. The emphasis has moved from organizing this factor of production on the basis of division of labour to organizing workers in teams and identifying and developing competencies. As Katzenbach and Smith (1992) write:

> None of this is new. Ancient generals understood the wisdom of teams no less than do modern corporate leaders. What makes that wisdom of such importance now – and so worth the urgent attention of top management – is not novelty but the proven link between teams, individual behavioural change, and high-performance. Building organisations that consistently outperform their competitors, as well as the expectations of their key constituencies (customers, shareholders, and employees), over an extended period of time requires lasting behavioural change. And experience shows that the same team dynamics that boost performance also enable such change – and do so far more effectively than can larger organizational units or individuals left to their own devices.
>
> *Source*: Reprinted with permission of the publisher from Jon R. Katzenbach and Douglas K. Smith, 'Why teams matter'. *The McKinsey Quarterly*, 1992 Number 3, p. 4. Copyright 1992 McKinsey & Company. All rights reserved.

New economics has to take this phenomenon on board and incorporate it within its discipline.

Goodbye pyramid – welcome spaghetti structure

Team work, and especially cross-functional teamwork, has become important because of the need for organizations to become lean in order to respond to market conditions. In traditional organizations based on the principles of organization put forward by Henri Fayol, work is divided into functions. Organizations established hierarchies on the basis of the division of labour and implemented the functions of planning, organizing, directing and controlling.

Max Weber, a German sociologist and one of the management thinkers, highlighted the merits of bureaucratic organizations. He theorized that the basic form of an organization was analogous to a pyramid. This pyramid incorporated different layers of management with specific functions and control procedures. The work was divided into functions, then departments and tasks. The chain of command went up and down the functional ladder.

The pyramid structure of organizations has been with us for over two hundred years. In the late 1980s some organizations began to question the appropriateness of the pyramid structure in making organizations flexible enough to meet market needs. In the context of doing business in the 1990s, some organizations found the pyramid structure too costly, and too slow to adapt and respond to business and market needs.

Gradually organizations like General Electric, Royal Insurance and Asea Brown Boveri (ABB) began to delayer their organizations and flatten the structure. *Business Week* (17 October 1994) indicated that in moving to flatten management structures, Europe – particularly Britain, Scandinavia and the Netherlands – was moving fastest.

A horizontal structure facilitates the organising of work around processes which link to customer needs, instead of around functions or tasks. It also allows team working within organizations.

Frank Ostroff and Douglas Smith (1992) write on the theme of the horizontal organization:

> In this alternative form of organization, work is primarily structured around a small number of business processes or work flows, which link the activities of employees to the needs and capabilities of suppliers and customers in a way that improves the performance of all three. Work and the management of work get performed more by teams than by individuals, and these teams assume real managerial responsibilities. In fact, flatter, but still hierarchical, arrangements of teams replace the steeper, more vertical hierarchies of traditional functional management.
>
> At the same time, the evaluation, decision-making and resource allocation aspects of management shift toward a focus on continuous improvement. That means information and training get provided just-in-time – on a 'need to perform', not a 'need to know', basis. Career paths

follow work flows: advancement goes to people who master multiple jobs, team skills, and continuous improvement. Compensation rewards both individual skill development and team performance.

Many organizations are transforming themselves not to maximize profits but to remain in business and compete effectively. Some have transformed themselves by eliminating formal structure as such. Andrew Eames (1998) gives the example of a company known as Oticon which specializes in making hearing instruments. This company is based in Copenhagen and they have been trading since 1904. Their turnover is in the region of £78 million.

> *A horizontal structure facilitates the organising of work around processes which link to customer needs, instead of around functions or tasks.*

Oticon have removed all layers of management and instead have created what the Oticon president calls a spaghetti structure. Staff have no designated desks; they perform a multi-job function; there are no traditional job specifications, no regulated hours, and no reports. The company believes that its staff are more interested in challenging and exciting tasks than in formal status and titles.

Reengineering

In the 1990s attention switched from systems to processes. In 1995 Michael Hammer and Jim Champy published a book with the title *Reengineering The Corporation* in which they advocated a radical redesign of an organization's processes in order to improve productivity and overall performance. Turning Adam Smith's theory of the division of labour upside down they turned their attention to reinventing the organization by focusing on processes.

Hammer and Champy stressed that the change must be fundamental and radical, the focus should be on process and the improvements must be dramatic. Process orientation will lead to improvements in quality, cost service and cycle time. Many organizations like Kodak, IBM Credit Corporation, the National and Provincial Building Society, Continental Canada Insurance and Hall Mark, including some in the not-for-profit sector, embarked upon reengineering their businesses.

> *What has enabled organizations to transform their processes has been the availability of sophisticated computers and improvement in information technology.*

The most quoted example of process reengineering is the accounts receivable operation of the Ford Motor Company. The operation once employed 500 people shuffling purchase orders and invoices among themselves. Now 125 people do the same job faster. The clerk at the receiving dock, using a computer to reconcile orders instantly, is authorized to accept orders and issue payment. No more paper shuffling! What has enabled organizations to transform their processes has been the availability of sophisticated computers and improvement in information technology.

Reengineering principles involve the integration of various tasks and activities into one, work is performed where it makes most sense, non-value added activities are eliminated, functional silos and functional stovepipes are removed and, most importantly, core processes are aligned to business strategy.

The example of the Ford Motor Company was similar in impact to that of the pin making factory of Adam Smith. Reengineering business processes brings about economies in operations which in turn affect the production possibility frontier at micro and macro level.

Economic principles and models have to take into account business reality. In the next few chapters we will highlight other business initiatives which impact upon market forces and economic analysis.

All things are not equal

In economics there are three broad sets of assumptions. The first set relate to the behaviour of consumers. It is assumed that consumers seek the greatest satisfaction from spending their money. The second set relate to the behaviour of business people (entrepreneurs). Here it is assumed that the main aim of every entrepreneur is to make as much money as possible. The third set relate to the physical structure of the world.

According to Stonier and Hague (1961);

> Assumptions are about geography, biology and climate. Assumptions in this group are usually implicit rather than explicit, but an attempt is made to ensure that economic theory asks nothing which is physically impossible. For example, when economic theorists discuss agricultural problems they acknowledge that harvest time is determined by nature. The economist has to accept this as a fact. Again, no reputable economist would put forward a theory based on the assumption that bananas and grapes grow in profusion in Scotland. Similarly, economic analysis accepts the fact that industrial workers need a given amount of rest each day, and that technical conditions prevent industrial output being unlimited in amount.

Advancement of science and technology has weakened the assumptions which form the basis of economic analysis. The way business is done has changed significantly and the nature of organizations is changing very dramatically. Economists have to consider the implications of these changes in order to refocus and fine-tune their principles and models. What causes the wealth of nations now has significantly changed from the causes identified by Adam Smith more than two hundred years ago.

VERDICT

How can these assumptions be sustained in a period where very intensive and dramatic changes are taking place in the business world? Economic principles and models need to be constantly monitored, fine-tuned and transformed to make them meaningful to business executives. Economic and technological convergence will and is changing the way wealth is created nationally and transnationally. Information infrastructure is developing to facilitate effective diffusion of knowledge and innovation. Increasing convergence will impact the economic bases of all countries involved and affected by the globalization process.

EXECUTIVE SUMMARY

- Economic principles and models are undergoing significant transformation in an ever-changing business world. Economists have to wake up to this transformation.

- The business world is witnessing 'the death of distance' and the convergence of technologies which in turn force organizations to adopt various initiatives in order to gain and retain competitive advantage.

- The globalization process is changing the way businesses are conducted and is accelerating the diffusion of know-how and innovation.

- Globalization is here to stay. Its implications are affecting economic concepts and models. If economics is to be meaningful to business executives, economists have to face the challenge of redefining economic concepts and principles.

- The selected four tenets in economics – namely, the law of diminishing returns, the tendency to increasing returns, the production possibility frontier and the division of labour – are examined and explored within the context of the modern business environment.

- The relevance of the law of diminishing returns is decreasing significantly, whereas the tendency to increasing returns will gain prominence due to high-tech industries.

- The production possibility frontier as a model reflects the concept of 'opportunity cost' and the subject matter of economics but its validity in practice is questioned.

- The division of labour gained considerable significance during the industrial revolution and it underpinned subsequent business organizations. In the 1990s, the introduction of cross-functional teams, the flattening of organizational structures and the reengineering of business processes have undermined the importance of the division of labour.

References

Aley, James (1996) 'The theory that made Microsoft', *Fortune*, 29 April, 23–4.

Drucker, Peter (1986) 'The changed world economy', *Foreign Affairs*, 64 (4), 768–91.

Eames, Andrew (1998) 'Now for something completely different', *Business Life*, February 1998, 54–7.

Hammer, Michael and Champy, Jim (1995) *Reengineering The Corporation*, London: Nicholas Brealey.

Katzenbach, Jon R. and Smith, Douglas K. (1992) 'Why teams matter', *The McKinsey Quarterly*, 3, 4.

Kotler, Philip (1994) *Marketing Management*. 8th edn. Prentice Hall, 12–13.

Kurtzman, Joel (1998) 'Thought leader: W. Brian Arthur', *Strategy & Business*, second quarter, 98–9.

Lewis, William W. and Harris, Marvin (1992) 'Why globalization must prevail', *The McKinsey Quarterly*, 2, 115.

Naisbitt, John and Aburdene, Patricia (1990) *Megatrends 2001*, London: Sidgwick & Jackson.

Ostroff, Frank and Smith, Douglas (1992) 'The horizontal organization', *The McKinsey Quarterly*, 1, 151–2.

Sasseen, Jane (1994) 'The winds of change blow everywhere', *Business Week*, 17 October 1994, 54.

Stonier, A. W. and Hague, D. C. (1961) *A Textbook of Economic Theory*. Harlow: Longman.

Gateway Two

DEMAND AND SUPPLY
Let's get real

I've given up trying to be rigorous. All I'm concerned about is being right.

Stephen Hawking

INTRODUCTION

Demand and supply in economics constitute two key levers of price mechanism. The interaction of demand and supply determines prices. At the heart of price mechanism lies the concept of consumer sovereignty.

In the past few years consumer needs and expectations have been globalized and the sovereignty of national consumer culture has been replaced by cross-cultural consumer sovereignty. At the same time, the concept of supply, as presented in economics, has been diffused due to outsourcing and the capability of technology to integrate the complete value chain.

How should we view the concepts of demand and supply within the modern business context? Is it possible and necessary to view demand and supply as mutually exclusive areas? Can consumers assume the characteristics of suppliers? If so, what are the implications for businesses?

DEMAND

According to the law of demand, in the market for any goods the quantity of those goods demanded by buyers will tend to increase as the price of the goods decreases and will tend to decrease as the price increases, assuming all other things remain equal (*see* Fig. 2.1).

What consumers demand and what they want are two different things in economics. What they want may be outside their financial limit. In other words, they cannot afford to buy what they really want. Demand in economics, therefore, is effective demand – that is, demand backed by money.

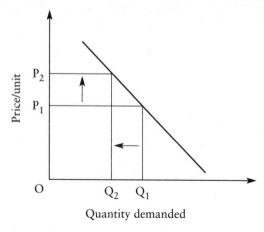

Fig. 2.1 The law of demand

This law is underpinned by the theory of diminishing marginal utility. Utility in a sense is equivalent to consumer satisfaction. If a family did not have a television then the acquisition of the first television will yield some degree of utility (satisfaction). Acquiring a second television, as some households now do, will increase the total utility but the utility derived from the second television will be less than the utility derived from the first. In other words, the marginal (additional) utility of the first television is greater than the utility derived from the second. A third television may increase total utility but the marginal utility of the third television will be less than the marginal utility of the second. Eventually the total utility of acquiring more televisions will fall (*see* Fig. 2.2).

The law of diminishing marginal utility underpins the law of demand and causes the demand curve to slope downwards from left to right.

When the price of a journey to Paris by Eurostar falls, more people will travel to Paris by Eurostar because:

● travel to Paris by other modes of transport, such as by bus or plane, will become relatively dearer;

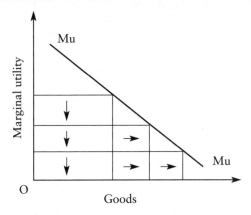

Fig. 2.2 The theory of diminishing marginal utility

- the fall in price will put the journey within reach of those travellers who could not afford to travel to Paris by Eurostar;
- existing travellers may make more frequent journeys to Paris by Eurostar.

Differences between demand and quantities demanded

This aspect of economics has always been confusing to many students. Quantities demanded of any product change as a result of price changes. Price alone is a driving factor. In Fig. 2.1 when the price of, say, beef falls from P_2 to P_1, the quantity demanded of beef increases from Q_2 to Q_1. If the price goes up to P_2 again, the quantity demanded falls from Q_1 to Q_2. The demand curve as such does not shift. All the changes in the quantities demanded for beef take place along the curve.

Change in demand brings about the shift in the demand curve. The demand curve in Fig. 2.1 will move to the right of the existing position. What brings about the shift in the demand curve?

- Changes in consumer preferences may shift the demand curve. If a consumer prefers to eat chicken instead of beef, this consumer's demand curve for beef will shift downwards, to the left of the existing position.
- Expectations also affect the demand for a product. If consumers expect the price of beef to increase permanently then this will have an impact on demand.
- Substitutes will affect the demand for many products. Demand for specific vegetables or fruit has changed as a result of the availability of a range of vegetables and fruit from other countries.

The theory of demand is based on the assumption that consumers have a scale of preferences. Economists feel that consumers' demand would be too erratic for them to construct a theory of demand unless preference scales were to some degree rational and stable through time and purchases were made in accordance with them.

In practice, consumers' scale of preference is influenced and in some cases manipulated by advertising. Advertising has become one of the critical tools of the marketing mix. Many companies use advertising to provide information about their products and to persuade consumers to buy their brands. Advertising is conducted via newspapers, television, radio, bill boards and now the Internet. According to *The Economist*, the Internet has already connected 50–60 million of the world's people through a seamless digital network. Where they live and what time zones they are in make no difference. Dell Computer is selling $1 million worth of PCs a day on the web.

Advertising is used to introduce new products to the market, to inform customers of special attributes of a particular product or brand, to communicate with remote consumers or where the manufacturers and suppliers want to persuade potential consumers to buy a product.

Marketers use celebrities to endorse their products. Adidas, Nike and Reebok use well-known athletes to promote their products thus influencing consumers' choice. Coca-Cola and Pepsi Cola use pop stars to reinforce their products' appeal to young consumers.

According to marketing guru Philip Kotler (1994), the main objectives of advertising are the following:

To inform

Telling the market about a new product	Describing available services
Suggesting new uses for the product	Correcting false impressions
Informing the market of a price change	Reducing buyers' fears
Explaining how the product works	Building a company image

To persuade

Building brand preference	Persuading buyers to purchase now
Encouraging switching to your brand	Persuading buyers to receive a sales call
Changing buyers' perception of product attributes.	

To remind

Reminding buyers that the product may be needed in the near future	Keeping it in buyers' minds during off-seasons
Reminding buyers where to buy it	Maintaining its top-of-mind awareness

Source: Philip Kotler, *Marketing Management* (1994) 8th edn, p. 629. Reprinted by permission of Prentice-Hall, Inc. Copyright 1994.

From these objectives it can be seen that the consumer's scale of preference and buying behaviour is significantly influenced.

According to Warren J. Keegan (1974):

An intriguing question for international marketers that has not yet been empirically studied is the marginal efficiency of advertising expenditures in economics at different stages of economic development. Is a marginal dollar of advertising in Argentina, where the receptiveness to the additional advertising message is presumably higher than that in the United States, greater than the marginal expenditure of a dollar of advertising in the United States? From the point of view of the international advertising manager to optimise his or her global expenditure of advertising revenues, this is an important question.

The Economist (1998) states:

In the economist's view of the world there is little need for firms to spend so much money cajoling consumers into buying their wares. Of course, people need good information to make good choices, and it is often too costly or time-consuming to collect it themselves. So advertising a product's features, its price, or even its existence can provide genuine value. But many ads seem to convey no such 'hard' information. Moreover, most advertising firms place a huge emphasis on creativity and human psychology when designing campaigns.

Economists need to explain, therefore, why a rational consumer would be persuaded by an ad which offers nothing but an enticing image or a good laugh. If consumers are rational they should ignore such obvious gimmicks. If producers are rational they should not waste money on ads that consumers will ignore. The existence of such advertising thus stands out like a giant billboard, proclaiming to economists that something is amiss.

The changing nature of consumer behaviour

Economists assume, in explaining the theory of demand, that consumers are rational and that the context within which they make decisions is static. The rationality issue will be examined later in this chapter but it is important to note that the dynamics of consumer behaviour are changing dramatically. This would affect the decision-making process.

Susan P. Douglas and C. Samuel Craig (1997) write:

Radical changes are taking place in the forces moulding consumer behaviour. These dramatically impact the patterning of markets, the formation of consumer tastes and preferences, their information seeking and purchase behaviour, and the diffusion of new products and ideas. In the first place, massive waves of migration are taking place, as consumers from emerging market economies are moving to industrialised economies. The largest diaspora is that of the Chinese who are spreading throughout Asia as well as moving to the US and Europe. The next largest movement is that of Latin America, notably Mexico and Colombia into the US. Waves of migration into Europe are also taking place, as Turks migrate to Switzerland and Germany, Arabs move from North Africa to France, and Indians and Pakistanis move to the UK.

Secondly, consumers are becoming more mobile and travelling more both for pleasure and business. As a result they are becoming exposed to the products, lifestyles and behaviour patterns of consumers in other countries. This trend is becoming particularly marked within regions, as barriers come down, and consumers and goods move freely across national boundaries.

Changing patterns of interpersonal and socio-cultural communication, spawned by easier travel, satellite communication links, the Internet, etc., have generated an increasingly complex patterning of consumer behaviour . . .

Source: Reprinted from Susan P. Douglas and C. Samuel Craig, 'The changing dynamic of consumer behaviour: implications for cross-cultural research', *International Journal of Research in Marketing*, Vol. 14 No. 4, pp. 380–381. Copyright 1997 with permission from Elsevier Science.

Since consumer behaviour underpins the concept of demand, the changes highlighted by Douglas and Craig have to be considered in reformulating the concept of demand.

┌─────────────────────────┐
│   **VERDICT**   │
└─────────────────────────┘

Whichever way one looks at the effect of advertising in economics, advertising constitutes one of the factors affecting change in demand and, as a consequence, it impacts the demand curve of a product.

As far as consumer behaviour is concerned, the scale of preference is not as simple as presented by economists. The sovereignty of national consumer culture is disappearing and being replaced by cross-cultural consumers. Economics has to recognize this change.

Hicks (1946) writes:

The pure theory of consumer's demand, which occupied a good deal of the attention of Marshall and his contemporaries, has received far less notice in the present century. The third book of Marshall's Principles *still remains the last word on the subject so far as books written in English are concerned. Now Marshall's theory of demand is no doubt admirable, but it is remarkable that it has remained so long upon such an unquestionable eminence. This would be explicable if there were really no more to say on the subject, and if every step in Marshall's analysis were beyond dispute. But this is clearly not the case; several writers have felt very uncomfortable about Marshall's treatment, and it is actually the first step, on which everything else depends, which is the most dubious.*

PRICE ELASTICITY OF DEMAND – LET'S NOT THROW THE BABY OUT WITH THE BATH WATER

Price elasticity of demand is defined as consumers' responsiveness to price changes. If the price of a commodity drops by 10 per cent, according to the law of demand, quantities demanded will increase.

But the question is: 'Will the quantities demanded increase by 10 per cent or more or less than 10 per cent?' If the quantities demanded increase by more than 10 per cent the commodity in question is said to have *elastic demand*. If they increase by less than 10 per cent it has *inelastic demand*, and if the quantities demanded increase by 10 per cent then it has *unit elasticity*.

Revenue implications

If the commodity has elastic demand then a decrease in price will increase quantities demanded proportionally more than the decrease in price. As a consequence, the firm's total revenue will increase. If, on the other hand, the price is increased, the quantities demanded will fall, again proportionally more than the increase in price, and the firm's total revenue will decrease (*see* Fig. 2.3).

Price/unit	Quantities demanded	Total revenue (£s)
10	100	1000
8	150	1200
12	80	960

Fig. 2.3 Elastic demand

Changes in price and changes in total revenue are inversely related.

With inelastic demand, if the price decreases, the quantities demanded will still increase but the increase will be less than proportional to the decrease in price. The firm's total revenue will decrease. If the price increases, the quantities demanded will decrease but the decrease will be less than proportional to the increase in price. The firm's total revenue will increase (*see* Fig. 2.4).

Price/unit	Quantities demanded	Total revenue (£s)
10	100	1000
8	120	960
12	90	1080

Fig. 2.4 Inelastic demand

The relationship between price and total revenue is direct.

With unit elasticity, price changes will affect quantities demanded but the firm's total revenue will remain the same.

Why is the price elasticity concept useful?

Because it has implications for total revenue, a firm should be aware of strategy in relation to price changes. As we have seen a decrease in price could lead to a decrease in total revenue and an increase in price could lead to an increase in revenue if the commodity has inelastic demand.

This means that a firm can practise price discrimination by charging a high price in a market where the commodity has inelastic price demand and a low price in the market where the commodity has elastic demand, thus maximizing its total revenue. In practice we have examples in the utility sector. For example, demand for telephone calls is inelastic during the day time and elastic during the night time. Therefore, a firm can introduce differential tariffs to the same group of consumers ; and this happens. There are many examples of price discrimination in the domestic market and in the international trade market. The motive is not always maximizing total revenue. For example, very often the dumping of goods takes place in order to gain market share in that particular country.

Price elasticity of demand depends on:

● the number of closeness of substitutes

- the proportion of income the commodity in question accounts for
- whether the commodity is a necessity or a luxury.

It is a relative concept in practice depending on the groups of consumers one considers and the demarcation of substitutes. The concept of necessity and luxury is changing constantly and the globalization process is facilitating this change. Privatization and deregulation of certain services, for example telecommunications, are also affecting elasticities of goods and services.

The concept of elasticity of demand and supply is also useful in forecasting prices. Bill Barnett (1993) explores the main factors that influence prices:

> A special challenge is presented by industries where demand and/or supply are inelastic – industries where prices are inherently volatile because it is hard for demand or production to respond to price changes, or takes a long time. The world oil market in 1986 is a good example. The Saudis increased production to discipline other world oil producers. They expected prices to fall from $26 per barrel to around $17, but in fact prices plummeted to $9.50. Why?
>
> First, demand was inelastic. Even when prices were much lower than usual, people had no practical way of using their cars significantly more or consuming much greater quantities of energy in industrial settings.
>
> Second, production was inelastic. Most oil-producing countries increased production as prices fell to maintain their total revenues and support their national economies. While some high-cost producers shut down (in West Texas, for example), their impact on total world production was small.
>
> If your industry, like oil, is inelastic, your need to forecast price will be high because prices can move dramatically in a short timeframe. Equally high is the need for scenarios to reflect the inherent uncertainties in some of the drivers of price levels. It is no surprise that Shell was an early leader in the development of scenario-based planning.

Price elasticity will remain a useful concept in economics. What will change will be the scope of the factors affecting price elasticity of demand as a result of the globalization of consumers' tastes and preferences.

VERDICT

Price elasticity is an interesting and useful concept and in theory it lends itself to measurement. In practice, however, when one deals with a significant number of commodities and diverse services offered domestically and internationally, it becomes very difficult to put the concept into practice. This baby should not be thrown out with the bath water because, as illustrated, it has its usefulness in some sectors in maximizing revenue and practising price discrimination.

THE LAW OF SUPPLY

As a general rule, when the price of a commodity falls the quantities supplied decrease and when the price increases the quantities supplied increase (*see* Fig. 2.5). High prices encourage more suppliers to enter the market, as a result of which total supply in the market increases.

What will change will be the scope of the factors affecting price elasticity of demand as a result of the globalization of consumers' tastes and preferences.

Like demand, there is a difference between the changes in the quantities supplied and the changes in supply. Changes in the quantities supplied come about because of changes in price, whereas changes in supply (shifting of the supply curve) come about because of changes in

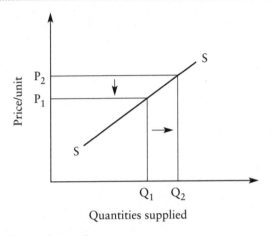

Fig. 2.5 The law of supply

costs, technological development, work practices, weather conditions, taxes, subsidies etc.

Supply is ultimately determined by cost. In economics emphasis is put on the relationship between average and marginal cost. In the next chapter the validity of these costs, and especially marginal cost, will be examined.

Supply – who is a supplier?

Economics does not tell us much about the nature of suppliers; the subject focuses its attention on the concept of supply and its relation to price and suppliers are presented as *entrepreneurs*. The types of supplier such as a monopolist, a duopolist and an oligopolist are dealt with in relation to the types of competition. Economics examines how they behave in relation to supply and price operating under different market structures.

In reality, even the concept of a supplier is difficult to define. As shown in Fig. 2.6, there are suppliers who provide goods to manufacturers, who in turn supply goods to their distributors and dealers, who in turn supply to customers and consumers.

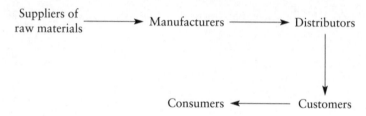

Fig. 2.6 Supply chain

Some manufacturers feel this structure is cumbersome if they want to deal directly with the customers. Joan Magretta (1998) writes about her interview with Dell Computer's Michael Dell:

> Michael Dell began in 1984 with a simple business insight: he could bypass the dealer channel through which personal computers were then being sold. Instead he would sell directly to customers and build products to order. In one swoop, Dell eliminated the reseller's mark-up and the costs and risks associated with carrying large inventories of finished goods. The formula became known as the direct business model, and it gave Dell Computer Corporation a substantial cost advantage.
>
> The direct model turned out to have other benefits that even Michael Dell couldn't have anticipated when he founded his company. 'You actually get to have a relationship with the customer,' he explains. 'And that creates valuable information, which, in turn, allows us to leverage our relationship with both suppliers and customers. Couple that information with technology and you have the infrastructure to revolutionise the fundamental business models of major global companies.'
>
> Dell is using technology and information to blur the traditional boundaries in the value chain among suppliers, manufacturers and even users. In so doing, Dell Computer is evolving in a direction that Michael Dell calls virtual integration . . . Virtual integration harnesses the economic benefits of two very different business models. It offers advantages of a tightly coordinated supply chain that have traditionally come through vertical integration. At the same time, it benefits from the focus and specialisation that drive the virtual corporation. Virtual integration as Michael Dell envisions it, has the potential to achieve both co-ordination and focus. If

it delivers on that promise, it may well become a new organisational model for the information age.

This article illustrates clearly the integration of value chain in practice and the role played by development in technology.

INTEGRATION OF SUPPLY AND DEMAND

In order to be responsive to consumer demand, in some cases manufacturers have taken initiatives to control their supply chain and make an attempt to improve the way they forecast consumer demand. Some manufacturers 'allow' their customers to influence supply. Below are two cases which illustrate what is happening in the business world today.

> *Some manufacturers 'allow' their customers to influence supply.*

According to the above-mentioned article by Joan Magretta (1998), Michael Dell says:

> Boeing for example, has 100,000 Dell PCs, and we have 30 people that live in Boeing, and if you look at the things we're doing for them or for other customers, we don't look like a supplier, we look more like Boeing's PC department. We become intimately involved in planning their PC needs and the configuration of their network.

In the 1990s suppliers of goods and services have focused their attention on customer profitability, relationship, retention and loyalty. It is said that it costs a company five times as much to win a new customer as it does to retain an existing one.

For a supplier to estimate consumer demand there is a need for a mechanism to filter back accurate information from the marketplace. In practice, gathering information is very difficult. However, it is very

Suppliers of goods and services have focused their attention on customer profitability, relationship, retention and loyalty.

important for companies to make good efforts to gather information on the demand for their products.

The following information is quoted from the article 'Gerry gives attention to demand' (1997) and is presented here in the form of a case study.

Case study 1

A SUPPLIER TAKING CONTROL OF DEMAND

Gerry Baby Products is a leading supplier in the US of 'juvenile' goods such as child carriers and car seating, play centres, bathroom accessories and security gates and frames. Based in Colorado, its $150 million annual turnover includes overseas sales, a side of the business that is targeted for growth. Gerry is one of the six divisions within Huffy Corporation, a consumer products and services group which reported net sales in 1995 of $684.7 million.

In 1995, while markets were going soft, the company made a $2.8 million capital investment in its ability to shorten development time and bring new products more quickly to the marketplace. More than 40 new products were launched in the Christmas and New Year period.

But Gerry knew that good products and lots of them was no longer a recipe for success, however good its reputation. As consumers are offered ever more choice, not only between retailers but within the same store, even a product that best meets a consumer's needs will only sell if it is in stock and offering value. At the same time the stores which stock the product are looking to fund competitive pricing by driving down inventory levels and their associated costs.

Under the ever tightening pressure Gerry had become a master of reaction, developing systems and people capable of reacting swiftly to changing demand. Resources were made available throughout its functional departments to meet the need, including rewards and incentives for those who could make things happen. However, Gerry was paying a high price. Because of the premium on a missed sale it was insuring itself against shortages by carrying increased inventory levels of 20% or more on volatile lines. And the time, money and energy that could not be used elsewhere.

Compounding all this was a growing realisation that the company had no idea how much of its effort was necessary because it had no clear idea what the true demand was for its products. Demand forecasting was based on the sales department's consensus estimates, prepared a month in advance of the target period and presented as a product-based rather than account-based projection. Overall, forecast accuracy against actual orders by product category was less than 70%.

In many situations Gerry did not know whether changes in quantities demanded were due to changes in retailers' inventory policies or to consumer pull.

Faced with so many gaps in its knowledge the company undertook a review of its order fulfilment claims from consumer purchase through to product replenishment. 'Our objective was to make supply chain replenishment into a competitive advantage so that retailers choose us because we get to their shelves more quickly,' says Mr Gosh, quality, engineering and consumer relations manager.

Gerry reengineered their supply chain, incorporating measures to get the estimate of demand right, by getting access to customers' electronic data interchange point-of-sale transaction data. This allowed information to be transferred back and forth between Gerry and the retailers, but required persuading each customer to share the information. Gerry has also built up personal as well as electronic links with its customers.

In an increasing number of cases, this relationship is moving to the status of vendor managed inventory (VMI) where Gerry as the manufacturer assumes the role of the retail buyer in reviewing sales and stock data to control product ordering and supply. Gerry's VMI partnerships cover about 17 per cent of turnover, a proportion it aimed to increase to 50 per cent by the end of 1998. What makes retailers comfortable with a VMI arrangement is the benefit it can quickly deliver.

Order volatility is lower, shipment times more closely tied to demand and overall inventory can be reduced. A halving in order volatility, which Gerry claims to achieve where it is responsible for replenishment, can produce a similar reduction in inventory.

But the most tangible result for the company of reengineering its supply chain has been the boost to its bottom line.

Source: 'Gerry give attention to demand'. *European Quality*, Vol. 4, No. 2, 1997. Copyright 1997 European Quality Publications Ltd. Reprinted with permission.

In the Gerry Products case study a manufacturer has taken an initiative to transform its value chain in order to exercise some control over demand for its products. *This is a novel concept in economics.*

Customer-driven supply

Another example of how the distinction between manufacturer, supplier and customer is becoming blurred is well reflected in the article entitled 'Chain of command' (1997) which presents the following case study:

Case study 2

CUSTOMER-DRIVEN SUPPLY

How Rover customers build their own cars

Rover customers can order a 'made-to-measure' car, in effect, straight from the factory. Using a multimedia selection and ordering system known as Discus, and available as a computer terminal in Rover showrooms, Rover customers 'build' the car they want by keying in their exact requirements.

With the multimedia system, customers can browse through an electronic catalogue of all available models within a specified price range.

Or, if they already know exactly what they want, they can follow the build-to-order approach.

This includes everything from the colour to the seat fabric, engine size and external trim. A video clip of the car, in the customer's chosen colour, then appears on the screen with the price and details of when it can be delivered. If the customer orders the car, it is electronically added to the relevant factory's production schedule.

The new tool is part of Rover's answer to the conundrum facing car manufacturers the world over – how to move on from the mass-manufacturer model pioneered by Henry Ford to one that is tailored to a customer's specific requirements. In Ford's day, the quip was 'you can have any colour, so long as it's black'. Now, however, made-to-order is the Holy Grail for which carmakers are aiming.

Although made-to-order originated with the Japanese, Rover's multimedia tool is the first practical application in the UK that allows a customer to order a car direct from the factory electronically. Rover's eventual aim is to tie its suppliers into the system so that just-in-time delivery of components, from steering wheels to seats, can be triggered directly from customer orders.

In the case of Rover, customers (demand side) are able to dictate supply with the help of technology. Supply and demand, though still important levers in price mechanism, cease to be mutually exclusive as presented in traditional economics.

The era of electronic demand and supply

The interrelationship between demand and supply has become very complicated and diffused as a result of accelerated technological development. In some cases it is difficult to draw a demarcation line between manufacturers, suppliers and customers. Harrington and Reed (1996) write:

Much has been written about the opportunity to gather customer data through business-to-consumer electronic networks, and thereby not only improve customer service but also begin to 'lock in' particular segments by offering them more finely targeted products and services. Much less has been said, however, about the power of networks to destabilize relationships between vendors and suppliers in business-to-business markets. Access to a fuller range of information about product availability and pricing can shift power away from established relationships. The result may be reduced price to the vendor.

The way a number of companies, like NEC and others, have decided to open up their proprietary purchasing and materials databases illustrates precisely this point. For example, NEC has opened up its centralized purchasing control network that compares information from buyers in each division to identify the best prices and terms from each supplier. The new system will allow input via public networks from an unlimited number of component vendors and public databases, effectively leveling the playing field for NEC's suppliers. Traditional suppliers will no longer be able to rely on their access to buyers in order to remain the source of choice. For component companies that were not part of the original closed network, a whole new set of relationships becomes possible."

Source: Reprinted with permission of the publisher from Lorraine Harrington and Greg Reed, 'Electronic commerce (finally) comes of age' *The McKinsey Quarterly*, 1996, No. 2, p. 72. Copyright 1996 McKinsey & Company. All rights reserved.

Apart from integration of demand and supply, Harrington and Reed highlight the fact that modern technology also provides an opportunity for suppliers to 'lock in' particular segments of their markets, to effectively use the information relating to their customer base and to form networks among suppliers.

> *Customers (demand side) are able to dictate supply with the help of technology.*

Recently the development of call centres that integrate telecommunications and computer technology have made them the most effective instruments for closing the gap between the buyer (demand) and seller (supply) and moving the customer to the forefront of planning, development, production and delivery of goods and services. Call centres are also becoming gateways to virtual and real markets.

VERDICT

Supply and demand can no longer be looked at as two distinct and separate components. In the business world nowadays manufacturers, retailers and customers collaborate to integrate the supply and demand chain. This need arises as a result of competition and also because customers are becoming increasingly sophisticated and knowledgeable about goods and services they demand.

The distinction between demand and supply is becoming blurred, as witnessed in the cases of Dell and Gerry Baby Products. This integration is being accelerated by the development of electronic commerce.

DETERMINATION OF PRICES

The price of a commodity is determined by the interaction of demand and supply. Let us assume that the demand for and supply of mobile phones at any given time are as shown in Fig. 2.7, assuming all other things remain equal.

Price/unit (£s)	Demand (units)	Supply (units)	Comments
50	10	30	Supply in excess of demand
15	80	10	Demand in excess of supply
30	50	50	Equilibrium situation

Fig. 2.7

At £50 a unit demand will be 10 units and supply will be 30 units. Supply is in excess of demand and as a result the price of mobile phones will fall. At £15 per unit demand will be 80 units but supply will be 10 units. There will be an excess of demand over supply and the price will increase. Prices will fluctuate till demand and supply are equal at £30. The market is said to be at equilibrium. The equilibrium price will prevail until forces in the market (factors affecting demand and supply) come into play to disturb the equilibrium.

The futures and options market developed to stabilize price fluctuations and minimize risks.

To take an example from the foreign currencies market, let us assume there are two currencies in the market – pound sterling (£) and US dollars ($). If the demand for pound sterling increases due to a variety of reasons, then the price of US dollars in relation to pound sterling will fall. Pound sterling will be expensive and British goods as a consequence will become expensive (compared to American goods). This will affect the performance of British exports.

If, on the other hand, US dollars increase in demand, then dollars will become expensive in relation to pound sterling and this time American exports to the UK will fall because American goods will become expensive.

Interaction of demand and supply will affect prices so there will be fluctuations in prices and businesses will face uncertainties. In order to overcome or minimize such fluctuations different mechanisms are developed in different commodity sectors.

Futures and options

Futures markets are not new a phenomenon; they date back over five hundred years. The futures and options market developed to stabilize price fluctuations and minimize risks. In the futures market a contract binds the two parties involved to the sale or purchase of something at a specified future date, at a fixed price.

An option is an agreement under which the payment of a sum of money gives a right (but not an obligation) to buy or sell something at an agreed price by a specified date. A call option is the right to buy, a put option is the right to sell.

There are many examples in business of hedging mechanisms to stabilize prices of various commodities.

The role of futures markets

The role of futures markets is very clearly explained by Mark Britten-Jones (1997):

> Two basic approaches have been taken to explain trading in futures: the insurance approach and the liquidity approach. These roles are not separate but we shall examine them one at a time.
>
> The insurance approach takes as a typical participant a producer or user of a commodity. For example, a wheat farmer who is concerned about the risk of fluctuations in the price of wheat from now until his wheat is harvested may sell wheat futures contracts in order to lock in a price for wheat. By such an arrangement he can protect himself against falls in the wheat price that could result in bankruptcy, loan default and so on.
>
> A more modern example might be that of a corporate treasurer who knows he or she will need to borrow money in six months' time to finance a business expansion. By selling an interest rate futures contract he or she is able to hedge the company against rises in interest rates that may occur in the next six months.
>
> This approach distinguishes two types of participants in the futures markets: hedgers, such as the farmer and corporate treasurer in the examples above, and speculators, who have no position in the underlying but are participating in the futures market in the hope of earning profits from their speculative activities.
>
> The liquidity approach is perhaps a better explanation. It emphasises the

institutional features of futures markets that permit low transaction costs. The presence of contracts with well-defined terms, the performance guarantee of the clearing house and the book-entry accounting of open positions all reduce trading costs by centralizing search and credit activities.

This approach emphasizes demand for immediacy, which is the willingness to buy or sell now rather than wait. This demand depends on the volatility of the underlying price and the extent to which the underlying price affects the wealth of the buyer or seller.

The role of a futures market is not just to provide hedging capability but to provide it extremely quickly. For these reasons futures markets have been very successful for hedging price risk on markets in which intermediaries hold significant inventories and for which price volatility is high. Viewed in this light the incredible growth in financial futures is not surprising.

Futures markets constitute an interesting example of minimizing volatility of price changes.

Pricing in a business world – the rules have changed

The determination of market price is not as neat as suggested in economics. Demand and supply play key roles but the whole concept of demand and supply is complicated in practice. In many situations suppliers provide goods to manufacturers who in turn produce goods and send them to various distributors to sell them to customers.

> *The interaction of demand and supply has become extremely complex in a global context.*

The interaction of demand and supply has become extremely complex in a global context. Ram Charan (1998) highlights the influence of disinflation and the opening up of markets in Asia, Latin America and Eastern Europe with their currency devaluations on the pricing strategies of companies like IBM, Allied Signal and Ford.

Emerging markets have accumulated lots of foreign debt and lots of manufacturing capacity. To service the debt and to compete in export markets, they devalue their currencies thus boosting competition in export markets. Charan's article illustrates clearly how macroeconomic factors and global forces impact and drive strategies of many companies. It is not simply a question of the interaction of demand and supply.

Ram Charan goes on to emphasize the fact that global supply simply does not mean reducing prices to win customers. Many corporations, like General Electric, add value by meeting customer needs, for example by cutting response time.

Pricing services rather than goods

Demand, supply and the determination of prices in economics focus attention on goods rather than services. It is implied that services are no different from goods and that their prices are determined by the interaction of demand and supply. Economics does not help to explain the determination of prices of intangible goods – it is not a matter of straightforward interaction of demand and supply.

In practice it is difficult to price services because they are intangible products. Professor Leonard Berry of Texas A&M University and Manjit S. Yadav, assistant professor at A&M University (1996) discuss the implications of pricing intangible products in today's intensively competitive environment:

Unfortunately, little research exists on the pricing of services, and few people understand the special challenges involved. But services are a special breed of product, and marketers need to treat them as such. Services are performances; therefore, they are intangible. Goods, on the other hand, are objects; they can be seen and touched. Customers can see tangibles associated with service, such as the people who provide the service and the equipment, but they usually cannot see the service itself. This inherent invisibility creates conditions that are far from ideal for services marketers, but they need to consider it if they want to improve their pricing practices. Purchasers of goods acquire tangibles – a couch, a VCR, a necktie, tennis shoes, toothpaste. Purchasers of services incur an expense rather than add to their accumulation of goods. They might, for example, take a trip, visit the theatre, or get a haircut, but at the end of the day, their "market basket" is empty. Purchasers of goods buy ownership and use; purchasers of services buy only use.

Recognising this subtle but important distinction between tangibility and intangibility can provide useful clues to understanding customers' reactions to services prices . . .

The intangibility of services makes it more difficult for customers to compare prices. In supermarkets, prices are affixed to tangible products grouped by category, but the non-physical nature of services impedes price and product comparisons. Since the products are invisible, customers cannot easily see their costs. For example, they have no fast method for comparing AT&T, MCI, and Sprint long distance services or prices before deciding which to select. Thus intangibility accentuates the complexity of services prices for customers.

Services differ from goods in the degree to which they possess *search*, *experience*, and *credence* attributes, three categories that help marketers distinguish among products. Those that can be evaluated before purchase and use have *search* attributes, those that can be evaluated only after they have been used have *experience* attributes, and those cannot be fully evaluated even after use have *credence* attributes. In general, tangible products are more likely to possess search attributes, whereas services tend to be higher in experience and credence attributes.

The two authors then go on to suggest three different types of pricing strategies – namely, satisfaction-based pricing, relationship pricing and efficiency pricing. They believe that pricing must establish and communicate a clear association between the price and the service attributes that customers value.

Satisfaction-based pricing: Because there is a high degree of uncertainty involved in purchasing intangibles, companies can minimise uncertainty by providing service guarantees or pricing services related to benefits. For example, on an on-line service paying for the information received rather than on time connected. The other way of minimising uncertainty would be to charge a flat-rate price.

In some cases customers are not sure of the cost involved. For example in buying legal services, e.g. wanting a will prepared, or a trust set up or getting legal advice, customers do not know how much they are going to pay for these services. The perception often is that one has to pay an arm and a leg to get a service from any lawyer. Flat-rate pricing, deciding before delivery what the price would be, will eliminate or minimise uncertainty.

Relationship pricing. Some organisations reduce prices in order to establish a relationship with their customers. Marketers use long term contracts that offer customers price and non-price incentives in order to consolidate the relationship. 'Such contracts transform business transactions from relatively isolated events to a series of steady, sustained interactions.'

The other strategy is to provide 'price bundling' – selling one or more services bundled together.

Efficiency pricing: Understanding, managing, and reducing costs are the cornerstones of efficiency pricing. Some or all of the resulting cost savings are passed on to customers in the form of lower prices. To be effective, the leaner cost structure must be difficult for competitors to imitate in the short run. Furthermore, cost savings passed on to customers must genuinely enhance their value perceptions. A good example of efficiency pricing in the UK is Virgin's financial services.

According to Berry and Yadav (1996), businesses can assess their companies' pricing vulnerability by answering the following questions:

- Are our prices easy to understand?
- Do they represent genuine value to our customers?
- Does our pricing encourage customers to do more business with us and be loyal to us?
- Does our pricing reinforce customers' trust in our company?

● Does our pricing ease customers' uncertainty about the purchase decision?

Berry and Yadav (1996) then go on to assert that:

Enlightened services marketers may differ from one another on the specific strategies that they implement, but all agree on the goal: capturing and communicating value.

Source: Reprinted from 'Capture and communicate value in the pricing of services' by Leonard I. Berry and Manjit S. Yadav, *Sloan Management Review*, Summer, 1996, pp. 42–50, by permission of the publisher. Copyright 1996 by Sloan Management Review Association. All rights reserved.

Value for money

Price is not the same as value. Value is a subjective evaluation and is not necessarily the same as the price we receive for an item in exchange. We may place a value on an item for a variety of reasons, but in economics we only deal with the value the market places on a product which can conveniently be measured by its price. Price constitutes the most obvious indicator of the value of satisfaction derived from consumption of a product.

> *Price constitutes the most obvious indicator of the value of satisfaction derived from consumption of a product.*

In economics it is assumed that when consumers make a purchase, the fundamental questions that go over in their minds are: 'If we buy this, how much must we pay for it? Is it worth it? What alternatives shall we forgo? And what would be their value to us?'

Purchasing decisions by consumers are made on the basis of a scale of preferences and the total available resources. The most important concept in the theory of demand is that of the margin. What is this concept?

According to Marshall (1920) 'the part of the thing which he (the consumer) is only just induced to purchase may be called the *marginal purchase* because he is on the margin of doubt whether it is worth his while to incur the outlay required to obtain it.' A unit of commodity which a consumer is momentarily considering whether to buy is called a marginal unit. The significance of each marginal unit diminishes as more of a commodity is purchased.

According to Stonier and Hague (1996):

> . . . when the consumer considers if any unit of a good is worth buying, he (or she) is working out the *marginal significance* to him of the good he is wondering whether to buy, in terms of the good with which it is to be bought. He is considering what is the value of the marginal unit of the purchased good in terms of the good with which he buys it.

As more of any good is purchased, the utility (satisfaction/significance) consumers receive from it tends to fall; they will value it less highly and will be prepared to buy it at a lower price. This is referred to in economics as *the law of diminishing marginal utility*. There have been many attempts to measure utility but it has remained a subjective concept. This concept underpins the downward-sloping demand curve which all students of economics are familiar with.

The theory of diminishing marginal utility is based on the assumption that people are rational in their decision making and that they make choices as if they were solving complicated deductive equations that enable them to make the best possible decisions. Cognitive scientists have indicated to us that people's decision-making process is influenced by past experience and perceptions. The new model of economics has to take on board the inductive rather than the deductive nature of consumer decision making.

Ralph Leszinski and Michael V. Marn (1997) say:

> 'Value' may be one of the most overused and misused terms in marketing and pricing today. "Value pricing" is too often misused as a synonym for low price or bundled price. The real essence of value revolves around the *tradeoff* between the benefits a customer receives from a product and the price he or she pays for it.
>
> The management of this tradeoff between benefits and price has long

been recognised as a critical marketing mix component. Marketers implicitly address it when they talk about positioning their product vis-à-vis competitors' offerings and setting the right price premium over, or discount under, them. Marketers frequently err along the two dimensions of value management, however. First, they fail to invest adequately to determine what the 'static' positioning of their products on a price/benefit basis against competitors should be. Second, even when this is well understood, they ignore the 'dynamic' effect of their price/benefit positioning – the reactions triggered among competitors and customers, and the effect on *total* industry profitability and on the transfer of surplus between suppliers and customers.

To illuminate the nature and magnitude of this missed value-management opportunity, value needs to be defined properly. Customers do not buy solely on low price. They buy according to *customer value*, that is, the difference between the benefits a company gives customers and the price it charges. More precisely, customer value equals *customer-perceived* benefits minus *customer-perceived* price. So, the higher the perceived benefit and/or the lower the price of a product, the higher the customer value and the greater the likelihood that customers will choose that product . . .

This approach differs significantly from the marginal utility (marginal satisfaction/customer benefits) approach. Moreover, a lot is being written about a value a consumer attaches to a purchase. The concept of value in economics is based on the price/utility ratio which is characteristic of the value-for-money approach to value. Some psychologists believe value in practice involves cognitive and affective dimensions.

Value in economics also has another dimension. It is assumed that manufacturers created value while consumers destroyed value created in the process of consumption. Factors of production, therefore, were value creators and they were rewarded accordingly, while consumers were value destroyers.

Rafael Ramirez (1999) writes:

In the industrial economy, while less than 10 per cent of the industrial workforce assembled goods, assembly lines nonetheless symbolized industry. Their sequential, linear, unidirectional characteristics were conceptualized as 'value chain'.

The customer was at the end of the chain, after value was realized – though only for the producer. Today customers can no longer be depicted as being in a such a position.

Technological innovation allowing practices such as distributed processing or concurrent engineering render value creation less sequential and more interactive. Customers co-design what they buy. They co-define, and often co-manage, logistics and manufacturing. For example, Ford (the customer) and ABB (the supplier) jointly developed new paint shops.

As a result assets are much more liquid. A study I conducted between 1986 and 1993 with colleagues from SMG, a Swedish research and consulting firm, showed that innovative firms outconfigure others by more intelligently allocating tasks than their competitors. They do this across time zones, 24 hours a day, 365 days a year.

They free themselves from thinking of value in terms of chains. Instead, they see themselves enmeshed in a global constellation (or web, network, ecology) of economic actors, who may simultaneously be suppliers, customers or competitors.

For example, furniture manufacturer IKEA, one of the firms studied, convinced a Czech shirtmaker to supply it with armchair cushions. It helped it to select the right machines, finance them, train the workforce, choose raw material, suppliers and arrange delivery logistics. For IKEA, the shirtmaker is thus supplier and customer.

As the proportion of work done by each party evolves, each also becomes a (partial) competitor. And customers converting their living rooms into IKEA factories become IKEA's assembly workforce.

The result of such configurations by innovative entrepreneurs is that more value can be created per unit of time and/or space than ever before. Value here is co-produced by two or more actors, with and for each other, with and yet for other actors.

Such commercial reconfigurations invite us to rethink organisations and management practices inherited from the industrial era. More fundamentally, they invite us to rethink value creation itself.

VERDICT

In practice, however, the concept of utility or significance to a consumer has been transformed. Price is not the only indicator of utility. Consumers are now looking for (a) value for money, (b) delivery of service excellence, (c) quality, and (d) relationships with suppliers. The two fundamental questions 'modern' consumers are asking are: 'Do I get my money's worth? and 'Do companies appreciate my business?'

In addition, consumers themselves have become value creators along with the factors of production. Economics has to consider this development.

The economics of premium pricing

How do companies respond in practice to the needs of consumers and their changing concept of significance or benefits? Professor Leif Sjoblom of IMD (1997) writes:

> . . . With increased competitive pressures and ever shortening product life cycles, firms find it increasingly difficult to resist price erosion, and almost impossible to justify price increases. Yet, business offers many examples of companies that have successfully applied premium pricing in competitive markets. For instance, IBM was not a low cost producer nor did it have a superior product when it launched its personal computer. Yet customers showed they were willing to pay a price premium for the IBM PC because of the perceived benefits and comfort conveyed by the IBM brand name, and the company's ability to provide valuable services through its extensive after sales service network.
>
> It is well known that a product or service should be priced based on its

perceived benefits, or its perceived economic value to the end user. Therefore, it is surprising to note how few companies do a systematic analysis of how their end users value their product. The vast majority of firms fall into the convenient trap of 'cost-plus' pricing, or they simply just match the prices of competition, without making a real effort to understand how much the customer is willing to pay. This is poor management and companies would be well advised to take an enlightened, proactive approach to pricing.

Pricing freedom: within what parameters?

The pricing freedom of a company is determined by several factors: the value the customer expects to derive from the offering, the level of competition, the uniqueness of the product, as well as the power balance between suppliers and customers. The pharmaceutical industry is the case in point. For generic drugs, which are clearly not differentiated, the price level is primarily determined by competition. Prescription drugs, on the other hand, have a price potential limited almost exclusively by the value a customer (i.e. the doctor) puts on one drug versus another.

The IBM example described earlier shows that premium pricing may be viable even in highly competitive markets. Another example is Crown Cork & Seal – an American company that supplies cans for breweries and soft drink companies. . . . A soft drink company can use a wide range of packages, from aluminium and steel cans to PET bottles, and can normally choose from many suppliers for each type of package. If, in addition, the soft drink company happens to be large, say Coca-Cola, the can supplier does not have much room for manoeuvre in its pricing policy.

Companies have considerably more pricing flexibility with new products than with existing ones. Typically, new and unique products are priced at a substantial premium. As a product matures and becomes increasingly copied by competition, price levels tend to drop. Since the price ceiling is determined by the benefits the customer expects from the product, the first step in a pricing policy is to estimate the economic value of the new product for the client . . .

Value pricing as the basis for an enlightened pricing policy cannot be separated from a well thought through business strategy. Its potential consequences not only on the company's profitability but also on its market positioning and image are such that it makes senior management's keen attention, or even direct involvement advisable.

There is more to pricing than the interaction of demand and supply. Apart from considering the structure of the market and the nature of competition, pricing policy (mechanism) should consider the changing concept of consumer benefits, the shortening of product life cycles, after-sales service and the bargaining power of customers and suppliers.

VERDICT

Demand and supply are presented as distinct components in the price mechanism model. In practice, the distinction is increasingly becoming blurred as shown in the example of Dell and the Rover Group.

Equilibrium price in economics is a static concept. Whereas demand and supply play a critical part, in practice, price is the function of (a) the value consumers attach to the product aesthetically, emotionally as well as functionally, (b) the relationship between producers, suppliers and customers, (c) strategic alliances, (d) uncertainty and ignorance on the part of producers and suppliers, and (e) consumer behaviour.

EXECUTIVE SUMMARY

- The law of demand in economics is underpinned by the concept of the scale of preference which is influenced by advertising. If consumers are rational, as economics suggests, is there a need for suppliers to spend money on advertising?

- Consumer behaviour is changing dramatically due to mass migration and cultural diffusion. This impacts upon the scale of preference and consequently on consumer demand.

- Price elasticity of demand within the theory of demand is a practical concept which enables businesses to practise price discrimination and make forecasts.

- Interaction between demand and supply has become very complicated within the context of the global economy. The distinction between manufacturers, suppliers and customers has become blurred as a result of electronic intermediation and strategic partnerships.

- Determination of market price is not simply the interaction of demand and supply. It is based on many considerations including macroeconomic factors and global processes.

- Pricing in practice depends on the nature of the product supplied. Services with their distinct attributes are priced on different bases including uncertainty, relationship and efficiency.

- Do prices reflect value in practice? In economics value lies behind the concept of marginal utility. Value is simply value for money. Value in practice incorporates aesthetic, cognitive and practical considerations.

- Consumers in economics are presented as value destroyers, whereas factors of production – land, labour, capital – are presented as value creators. This assumption is now questionable. Consumers are thus presented as value creators.

References

Barnett, F. William Jr (1993) 'Taking the mystery out of tomorrow's prices', *The McKinsey Quarterly*, 4, 104.

Berry, Leonard I. and Yadav, Manjit S. (1996) 'Capture and communicate value in the pricing of services', *Sloan Management Review*, summer, 42–50.

Britten-Jones, Mark (1997) 'An introduction to futures markets: insurance, liquidity, immediacy', in *FT Mastering Management*. London: Financial Times Management, 96.

'Chain of command', (1997) *Customer Service Management Journal*, xvi, September, 25.

Charan, Ram (1998) 'The rules have changed', *Fortune*, 16 March, 79–81.

Douglas, Susan P. and Craig, C. Samuel (1997) 'The changing dynamic of consumer behaviour: implications for cross-cultural research', *International Journal of Research in Marketing*, 14 (4), 380–1.

'Gerry gives attention to demand,' (1997) *European Quality*, 4 (2), 28.

Harrington, Lorraine and Reed, Greg (1996) 'Electronic commerce (finally) comes of age', *The McKinsey Quarterly*, 2, 72.

Hicks, J. R. (1946) *Value and Capital*. 2nd edn. London: Oxford University Press. 11.

Keegan, Warren J. (1974) *Multinational Marketing Management*. 3rd edn. USA: Prentice Hall.

Kotler, Philip (1994) *Marketing Management*. 8th edn. USA: Prentice Hall. 629.

Leszinski, Ralf and Varn, Michael V. (1997) 'Setting value not price', *The McKinsey Quarterly*, 1, 99–100.

Magretta, Joan (1998) 'The power of virtual integration: An interview with Dell Computer's Michael Dell', *Harvard Business Review*, March–April, 59–60.

Marshall, A. (1920), *Principles of Economics*. 8th edn. 91.

Ramirez, Rafael (1999) 'Unchaining value in a new economic age', *FT Mastering Global Business*. London: Financial Times Management, 129–32.

Sjoblom, Leif (1997) 'How much is the customer willing to pay? An application of value pricing', *Perspectives for Managers*, May, 1–3.

Stonier, A. W. and Hague, D. C. (1996) *A Textbook of Economic Theory*. Harlow: Longman, 39.

'The money in the message', (1998) *The Economist*, 14 February.

Gateway Three

COMPETITION AND MARKETS

From strategy to action

To put your ideas into action is the most
difficult thing in the world.

Goethe

It is only when you are pursued that you become swift.

Anon

INTRODUCTION

The business world is facing fierce competition from all corners of the world. Competition in economics is categorized as perfect competition and imperfect competition. Within imperfect competition fall monopolies, duopolies and oligopolies. Business strategies focused on price and output.

In the real world the nature of competition has been very complex and organizations formulate their strategies to extend beyond price and output. Companies like Microsoft and Intel create their own rules of competition and governments in many countries, through their privatization and deregulation policies, have added new sources of competition.

In addition the simple concept of marketplace where buyers and sellers come together has been transformed to marketspace due to accelerated technological development in the field of computing and telecommunication.

TYPES OF COMPETITION

Economic theory looks at markets in equilibrium, but in practice the dynamics of competition affect the equilibrium position. This is acknowledged in economic teaching.

Competition is categorized in economics as:

- perfect competition
- imperfect competition
- oligopolistic competition
- monopoly.

Most businesses come under the category of oligopoly. Various measures are being taken by governments in different countries to transform monopoly and oligopolist market structures in order to increase competition. The regulatory structures are introduced to act as surrogate 'perfect competition'.

Perfect competition

The following are the key characteristics of perfect competition:

● there are many buyers and sellers in the market and they have no significant influence on the size of the market;
● the product each firm manufactures is homogeneous – Product 'A' manufactured by various firms operating in a perfectly competitive market is the same in consumers' eyes;
● there is a perfect knowledge among buyers and sellers so there is no market manipulation;
● there are no barriers to entry into markets.

In these circumstances all firms are *price-takers*, which means that they have to accept the price prevailing in the marketplace.

The demand curve of a firm operating in a perfectly competitive market will be horizontal as shown in Fig. 3.1.

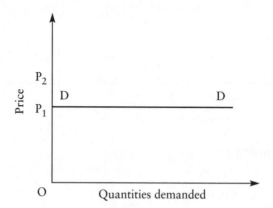

Fig. 3.1 A firm in perfect competition

A firm is a price taker. In this case the price of a commodity will be P_1. If this firm increases its price of the commodity to P_2, there will be no demand. The horizontal demand curve is the key characteristic of a perfectly competitive firm.

A perfectly competitive firm would have to be perfectly informed about all relevant present and future prices of its inputs and outputs. Likewise, a consumer would need to be perfectly informed about all present and future consumption possibilities.

Imperfect competition

In an imperfect competitive situation, there are many buyers and sellers as in perfect competition but some or all of the other conditions, such as perfect knowledge, homogeneity of product, do not exist. As a consequence, a firm in such a situation can influence market price.

The demand curve of a product for a firm in imperfect competition will be downward-sloping from left to right (*see* Fig. 3.2).

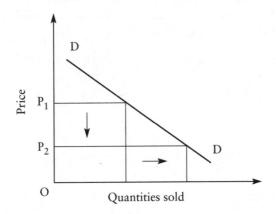

Fig. 3.2 A firm in imperfect competition

In order to attract more buyers this firm can reduce the price and sell more.

There are degrees of imperfection in the marketplace. The steepness of a demand curve for a firm in imperfect competition will depend on the degree of imperfections in the marketplace. The more imperfect the competition, the steeper the demand curve. Imperfection increases as:

- consumers have less and less information on product and/or price;
- goods become heterogeneous;
- collusions take place by suppliers in relation to production and price;
- more alliances and partnerships take place in practice.

Oligopolistic competition

The oligopolistic situation comes into existence when there are very few firms and each firm has to keep an eye out for its rivals' policies and marketing strategies. Like game players, they must take into consideration their competitors' strategies when formulating their own strategies and tactics.

Monopoly

A monopolist is a price-maker and has complete control of the market. A pure monopolist is a firm that accounts for 100 per cent of the sales in the market in relation to a specific product or service. Its demand curve will flow steeply downwards from left to right (*see* Fig. 3.3).

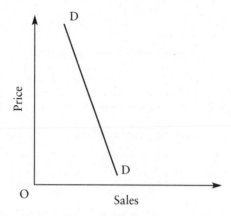

Fig. 3.3 A firm in a monopoly situation

Gateway Four will examine the costs and revenue situations of firms operating in a different competitive environment.

SOURCES AND NATURE OF COMPETITION

A competitive environment is the result of external and internal factors. These relate to the factors external or internal to companies and countries in which businesses operate. Externally and internally, businesses face competition from new entrants, suppliers and substitutes. According to Michael Porter, a strategy guru, there are five forces which create a competitive environment within which businesses operate. They are:

Externally and internally, businesses face competition from new entrants, suppliers and substitutes.

- barriers to entry
- pressures from substitute products
- bargaining power of buyers
- bargaining power of suppliers
- rivalry among current competitors (*see* Fig. 3.4).

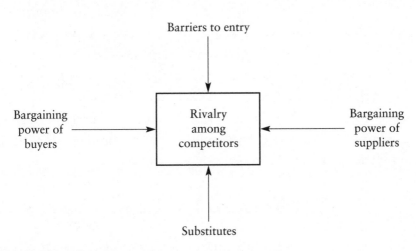

Fig. 3.4 Barriers to entry

Barriers to entry come about as a result of economies of scale (falling unit cost of production as volume of production increases), product differentiation, brands, customer loyalty, heavy capital cost of starting a new business, switching costs (one-off costs facing the buyer of switching from one supplier's product to another's), access to distribution channels, cost disadvantage independent of economies of scale (established costs which are not replicable by new entrants), government policy and regulations.

The intensity of rivalry among existing competitors depends on imperfections in the market (imperfect, oligopoly or monopoly competition). Competitors use varying strategies to make life uncomfortable for their rivals; these range from price competition and exclusive dealerships to strategic alliances and partnerships. Pressure from substitutes intensifies competition. This has become very prominent as a result of the globalization process.

> *Competitors use varying strategies to make life uncomfortable for their rivals.*

Substitutes now arrive from every corner of the world where competitors choose to source raw materials, labour and capital.

The bargaining power of buyers and suppliers also contributes to competitive pressures and influences firms' strategies. All five forces are interrelated.

Apart from various national and international forces that create competition, in the 1990s the policies of national governments have intensified competition. These policies have taken the form of privatization and deregulation. They have become major internal (coming from nations themselves) sources of competition.

Privatization and deregulation

In the 1980s and 1990s some countries, but especially the UK, have decided to privatize some of the industries under their control in order to enhance competition. The companies that went into the 'private sector' arena included British Telecom, British Gas, British Airways and British Steel. Water and electricity companies were broken into small regional units before they were privatized. Regulators were appointed to make sure that such 'privatized monopolies' did not exploit consumers.

The experience of privatization in the UK is very clearly explained by Alan N. Miller (1994):

> Privatisation is not merely a domestic issue. It is an integral part of the strategic renaissance which is taking place in many eastern and western European countries and in countries on other continents as well. It has already had a profound impact on the social, political, macroeconomic, and managerial dimensions of governments, government owned enterprises, and newly privatised firms. This impact is certain to increase and become even more widespread as governments further their efforts in this area and as other governments join the privatisation movement.
>
> World-wide interest in privatisation has increased recently for several reasons. These include 1. the collapse of communism in the former Soviet Union and its East European allies and the emerging governments' determination to transform state owned enterprises into private sector entities; 2. the desire of a growing number of political leaders and their constituents to reduce the size and scope of local and national government; 3. the problem of how governments can continue to provide adequate public services given the reluctance of many citizens to fund regular tax increases; 4. the commitment of some governments to increase public enterprises' efficiency, productivity, and responsiveness to customer needs; and 5. the desire of many nations to promote free market principles and to establish an enterprise culture. It is likely that other forces, including the need for governments to reduce their debt, promote competition in their nations' key industries, and encourage entrepreneurial activity, will sustain the keen international interest in privatisation through the turn of the century.

Privatisation in the UK

Whatever the causes of poor performance in the nationalised industries, the long-term results of the nationalisation programme in the UK are quite clear: lack of competition in important segments of the economy, limited choices for consumers, higher prices for goods and services sold by nationalised firms (which fuelled inflation nation-wide), customer dissatisfaction, low employee morale and productivity, political manoeuvring, management indecision, and economic stagnation.

To deal with the poor performance of nationalised industries both the Labour and Conservative Parties have over the years imposed standards and controls to provide an environment similar to a free market. Although these attempts sometimes were successful, they did not yield long-term solutions. Attempting to control the industries' behaviour by imposing surrogate market forces simply does not deal with the fundamental problem of State ownership. The privatisation programme which was initiated by the Thatcher government was a direct strategy to deal with the poor performance of the nationalised firms and with the social, political, macro-economic, and managerial problems associated with them.

For the Thatcher government, privatisation involved more than the transfer of state owned businesses to the private sector. It was part of the overall plan to create a truly free market economy in the UK. The reasons for and goals of the privatisation programme were to: 1. give consumers more choices, better service, and lower prices; 2. encourage more equal distribution of wealth by promoting greater ownership of corporate stock among employees and the general population; 3. decrease government control of business and lessen political interference in the management decision making process; 4. lower the national government's debt; 5. generate new tax revenues from privatised firms; 6. free government's funds to be used in sectors of the economy other than state owned businesses; 7. reduce the size of the government; 8. benefit the economy through higher returns on capital in the privatised industries; 9. stimulate managers to be more responsive to customer demands and to be more innovative in developing new products and services; 10. give employee shareholders a greater stake in their organisations, resulting in increased motivation and productivity; 11. enable managers to set organisational goals which are independent of the government's goals; and 12. allow competition to spur the efforts of manager and employees.

The privatisations which have been completed to date have involved: 1. the sale of all of a company's shares at one offering, 2. the sale of all of a company's shares at several separate offerings (which usually took place over a period of years), 3. the sale of some of a company's shares (with a government retaining a residual shareholding), and 4. the sale of either all or part of a company's subsidiary or of a major asset owned by the company . . . It is clear that businesses from virtually all industries (e.g. aerospace, automobile manufacturing, electricity generation, natural gas supply, oil exploration and production, and water supply), have been privatised.

When a monopoly in a particular industry is privatised, regulatory arrangements are made by the government to prevent extreme increases in prices and to ensure good customer service. For example, when British Telecom (BT) was sold to the private sector in 1984, a government regulatory agency (the Office of Telecommunications – OFTEL) was established to prevent BT from exploiting its monopoly position in the telecommunications industry. Furthermore, the government licensed Mercury Communications Ltd, a new telecommunications company, to compete with BT. Seven years after BT was privatised, a study by the International Telecom User Group found that despite competition from Mercury, BT still held a 95 per cent market share. It was also discovered that BT's customer pay significantly more for phone service than their American counterparts.

The British experience with privatisation seems to show that exposing industries to the financial disciplines of the marketplace generally creates better managed companies that produce higher quality goods and services and provide enhanced value to their customers.

Source: Reprinted from Alan N. Miller, ' Privatisation: lessons from the British experience', *Long Range Planning*, Vol. 27, No. 6, pp. 125–136. With permission from Elsevier Science.

Benefits of privatization

To summarize, privatization yields the following benefits:

- improved economic performance of previously state-owned enterprises
- greater responsiveness to the needs of the customers
- high returns on capital for enterprises
- improved operational efficiency
- improved incentives for management and employees
- more competition introduced into the economy
- more efficient pricing policies
- reduced government borrowing.

Privatization has now spread to many countries, for example in Latin America and Eastern Europe, where there is the political will to bring about socio-economic changes. In a situation where the size of the public sector is reduced, resources are 'freed' to the private sector which increases the size of the private sector (*see* Fig. 3.5).

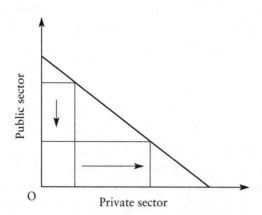

Fig. 3.5

Privatization and public interest

The new-found faith in privatization has spread to become the global economic phenomenon of the 1990s. John B. Goodman and Garry W. Loveman (1991) say:

> Refocusing the discussion to analyse the impact of privatisation on managerial control moves the debate away from the ideological ground of private versus public to the more pragmatic ground of managerial behaviour and accountability. Viewed in that context, the pro and cons of privatisation can be measured against the standards of good management – regardless of ownership. What emerges are three considerations:
>
> 1. Neither public nor private managers will always act in the best interests of their shareholders. Privatisation will be effective only if private managers have incentives to act in the best interest, which includes, but is not limited to, efficiency.
>
> 2. Profits and the public interest overlap best when the privatised service or asset is in a competitive market. It takes competition from other companies to discipline managerial behaviour.
>
> 3. When these conditions are not met, continued government involvement will likely be necessary. The simple transfer of ownership from public to private hands will not necessarily reduce the cost or enhance the quality of services.
>
> *Source*: Reprinted by permission of *Harvard Business Review*. From John Goodman and Gary Loveman. 'Does privatization serve the public interest?, *Harvard Business Review*, November–December, 1991, p. 28. Copyright 1991 by the President and Fellows of Harvard College; all rights reserved.

Goodman and Loveman shift the debate about privatization from an idelogical/political perspective to a business perspective. An efficiency mindset is going to constitute the main factor affecting the benefits of privatization.

Deregulation – the road to liberalization

The next wave of activity to enhance competition is deregulating certain industries. Regulatory frameworks come in many forms, such as intellectual property rights, privacy and data protection, competition law, consumer rights and industry regulation. The focus in this section is going to be on deregulation of industry.

Deregulation and liberalization of trade increase competition. The following are some of the most important activities which have taken place and are taking place in relation to trade liberalization:

- The much-publicized start date for the full deregulation of the telecommunications market in the European Union (EU) was 1 January 1998. This deregulation is aimed at boosting economic activity in the European Union. Technological progress is fundamentally changing the structure of the marketplace. Boundaries between traditionally distinct industry sectors are getting increasingly blurred as the process of convergence in the market intensifies.
- A global pact which liberalizes basic telecommunications came into effect on 5 February 1998.
- Internal US flights were deregulated in 1978 with the removal of regulations which caused barriers to entry; the industry quickly became more competitive. The number of airlines increased and fares came down which benefited consumers.
- The UK has begun to deregulate the airline industry. England and Wales have been liberalizing the gas market from the beginning of 1998.
- The 1992 Single Market involved a substantial degree of deregulation by providing a barrier-free market. The Single Market was officially launched in 1993; however, it is far from complete. The greatest problem areas are transport, public procurement and intellectual property. In December 1997 energy ministers reached a compromise agreement on rules for the internal market in natural gas. This follows the directive on the opening of the electricity market which was adopted in December 1996.
- In December 1997 the European Commission published its Green Paper on convergence which explored the opportunities for new

services such as home shopping and 'virtual business' – the term 'electronic commerce' is often used to embrace all these new services. The paper discusses the progress of deregulation to date, and suggests where more emphasis is needed in order to create this essential environment in which electronic commerce can flourish.

- The year 1997 saw the successful conclusion of the unfinished business of the 1986–93 Uruguay round of global trade talks relating to financial services. Negotiators from seventy countries finally agreed a deal on the liberalization of financial services. The ground-breaking pact covers over 95 per cent of the world's multi-trillion dollar financial services market involving $18 trillion in global securities assets, $38 trillion in international bank lending and about $2.5 trillion in worldwide insurance premiums.

MANAGING COMPETITION IN THE PRIVATE SECTOR – THE GAMES COMPETITORS PLAY

George Day and David Reibsten (1997) state:

Competition is a game as defined by game theorists where success depends on both our actions and the reactions of competitors, customers, partners, and their stakeholders.

These 'games' are becoming more difficult to play – or to win – as competition intensifies. Globalization and technological changes are spawning new sources of competition, de-regulation is changing the rules of competition in many industries, markets are becoming more complex and unpredictable, and information flows in a tightly wired world permit companies to sense and react to competitors at a faster rate.

This accelerated competition means it is no longer possible to wait for a competitor to make a move before deciding how to react. The new watchwords are anticipation and preparation for every eventuality. Every move of competitors is met with a rapid counter-move to ensure any advantage is temporary.

The most intense or hypercompetitive rivalries have spawned the cola wars where every move Coca-Cola makes is met by Pepsi Cola and every initiative by Pepsi is quickly countered by Coke. Today, every advertisement by MCI immediately stimulates a response by AT&T, and vice versa. The result is an advertising war in which collective annual spending has topped $1bn.

As soon as Kodak launches a new disposable camera, Fuji will have a similar model ready for the market. Even banks have launched credit card wars, where every offer of gifts or reduced charges is soon matched. No company can afford to let its rivals gain an obvious lead for long . . .

Okidata's mistake. As a case in point, in the 1970s Okidata produced an excellent dot-matrix line printer and won a significant share of the printer market. However, it did not take long for Hewlett-Packard to transform customers' perceptions of what a good printer was. First HP introduced an important inkjet model that had some advantages over Okidata's line. And, then it offered the Laserjets, a family of highly reliable printers based on a technological breakthrough that made them faster and quieter, that provided greater resolution, and even gave them substantial resale value.

Okidata complacently watched its share of the printer market rapidly erode while it continued to offer the customers 'the best damned (dot-matrix) printers in the market'. By stubbornly continuing to market a product that, compared with other available options, was no longer a wise investment for their customers, Okidata quickly lost its leadership position to Hewlett-Packard. Soon the new HP printers proved their worth in the workplace, and Hewlett-Packard captured the respect and loyalty of many of Okidata's former customers.

In a modern competitive environment complacency to consumer demand and taste will mean the market share of the companies involved will fall.

As a result of such fierce competition, many companies are trying different strategies to sustain their competitive strengths. In Gateway Four we will explore various strategic manoeuvres, such as alliances and partnerships, that are being formed by companies in different sectors.

One company and its competition

The story of one company, Intel Corporation, which has come up with a specific strategy to manage competition is told by Kathleen M. Eisenhardt and Shona L. Brown (1998).

THE STORY OF INTEL CORPORATION

Back in 1965, Gordon Moore, a cofounder of Intel Corporation, prophesied that the capacity of the microprocessor computer chip would double every 18 months. Moore's law, as it has since become known, may sound like a law of physics, but it's not. Instead, it's a business objective that Intel's engineers and managers have taken to heart. Over time, Intel has created a treadmill of new-product introductions that have set a blistering pace in its industry. In the decade between 1987 and 1997, Intel generated an astounding average annual return to investors of 44%. Even more impressive, recently Intel's annual earnings equalled those of the ten personal computer firms combined.

In a modern competitive environment complacency to consumer demand and taste will mean the market share of the companies involved will fall.

Although few companies will ever enjoy a market position like Intel's, managers can learn a key lesson from the world's premier chip maker. Intel is certainly the most visible – but by no means the only – practitioner of *time pacing*, a strategy for competing in fast-changing, unpredictable markets by scheduling change at predictable time intervals. Not only does Intel make Moore's Law a reality through its new-product introductions, but it also time-paces in other key areas. For example, about every nine months, Intel adds a new fabrication facility to its operations. CEO Andy Grove says, 'We build factories two years in advance of needing them, before we have the products to run in them and before we know that the industry is going to grow.' By expanding its capacity in this predictable way, Intel deters rivals from entering the business and blocks them from gaining a toehold should Intel be unable to meet demand.

Small and large companies, high and low tech alike, can benefit from time pacing, especially in markets that won't stand still. Cisco Systems, Emeron Electric, Gillette, Netscape, SAP, Sony, Starbucks, and 3M all use time pacing in one form or another. In rapidly shifting industries time pacing can help managers anticipate change and perhaps, like Intel, set the pace of change. But even in industries in which the rate of change is less than warp speed, time pacing can counteract the natural tendency of managers to wait too long, move too slowly, and lose momentum.

Instead of being reactive, the strategy which underpins 'the theory of the firm' in economics, companies have to be far more proactive in their thinking and implementation of their strategies.

Our understanding of time pacing emerged from almost a decade of research into the drivers of success in high-velocity, intensively competitive industries. One phase of the research took us inside 12 successful companies in different segments of the computer industry – an industry that serves as a prototype for this new competitive reality. We tested the relevance of these ideas in other industries as well, through targeted case studies and consulting work with executives. What we found is that wherever managers were coping with changing business environments, time pacing was critical to their success, helping them resolve the fundamental dilemma of how often to change.

Time pacing versus event pacing

For most managers, *event pacing* constitutes the familiar and natural order of things. Companies change in response to events such as moves by the competition, shifts in technology, poor financial performance, or new customer demands. Event pacing is about creating a new product when a promising technology comes out of the R&D laboratory, entering a new market in response to a move by a competitor, or making an acquisition because an attractive target becomes available. Managers who event-pace follow a plan and deviate from it only when performance weakens. In markets that are stable, event pacing is an opportunistic and effective way to deal with change. By definition, however, it is also a reactive and often erratic strategy.

In contrast, time pacing refers to creating new products or services, launching new businesses, or entering new markets according to the calendar. Even though time-paced companies can be extraordinarily fast, it is important not to confuse time pacing with speed. By definition, time pacing is regular, rhythmic, and proactive. For example, 3M dictates that 30 per cent of revenues will come from new products every year. Netscape introduces a new product about every six months, British Airways refreshes its service classes every five years, and Starbucks opens 300 stores per year to hit the goal of 2,000 outlets by the year 2000. Time pacing is about running a business

> *Companies like Intel have to come up with innovative strategies in order to become key players in an unpredictable market environment.*

through regular deadlines to which managers synchronise the speed and intensity of their efforts. Like a metronome, time pacing creates a predictable rhythm for change in a company.

Source: Reprinted by permission of *Harvard Business Review*. From Kathleen M. Eisenhardt and Shona L. Brown, 'Time pacing: competing in markets that won't stand still', *Harvard Business Review*, March–April, 1998, pp. 59–60. Copyright 1998 by the President and Fellows of Harvard College; all rights reserved.

The way organizations formulate their strategies and the way they behave is far more complex than the behaviour reflected in the 'theory of the firm' aspect of economics. Companies like Intel have to come up with innovative strategies in order to become key players in an unpredictable market environment. Instead of being reactive, the strategy which underpins 'the theory of the firm' in economics, companies have to be far more proactive in their thinking and implementation of their strategies.

VERDICT

In examining the economics of competition it has become important to consider the impact of privatization worldwide and the process of deregulation in constituting sources of competition. Privatization and deregulation accelerate the globalization process.

In the private sector companies formulate different strategies to manipulate competition. Time pacing is one of the ways to compete in the markets that won't stand still. Economics needs to accommodate such strategic manoeuvres in dealing with the topic of competition and assessing the behaviour of firms in different competitive situations.

THE MARKET ECONOMY – A MODEL OF PERFECTION!

Economists sketch market economy in the following way. Households sell resources (land, labour, capital, enterprise) to firms which make payments to households in the form of rent, wages, interest and profit. These constitute households' income. Households use their income to purchase goods from firms and the expenditure of households constitutes the income of the firms. Markets for consumers and markets for factors of production operate by means of demand and supply. Prices bring about transactions.

Many economists consider markets to be the key institutional feature of economic organization. Economic theory became synonymous with the analysis of the market economy. The neo-classical market economy is held by some economists to possess properties of optimality that make it superior to all other forms of economic organization. The competitive market economy is deemed by many economists to be at least as good as any other institutional alternative. Competition prevents businesspeople from exploiting consumers but it also acts as an efficiency mechanism to producers. According to Adam Smith, the force of competition acted as a kind of invisible hand to reconcile self interests and the common good in an orderly way.

Classical economists like Adam Smith took into consideration the dynamic forces of the marketplace. However, the dynamic aspect of the market was abandoned in the 1870s by the neo-classical economists; they focused their attention on the theory of price formation using the demand and supply mechanism within a static context.

Most resource allocation decisions are made by buyers and suppliers acting in markets. Markets play a significant role in determining what, how, and for whom goods and services should be produced. Markets transmit the knowledge needed to put the resources to required use. At the same time markets also act as a source of incentives. Consumers and the factors of production have an incentive to make use of the information with which market prices provide them.

FROM MARKETPLACE TO MARKETSPACE

The arrival of electronic markets

It has always been accepted in economics that there is no need for a market to be at a single place, building or location. According to economics, a market can equally consist of buyers and sellers who sit beside batteries of telephones in different buildings, as happens in the foreign exchange market. The only essential for a market is that all buyers and sellers should be in constant touch with each other, either because they are in the same building or because they are able to talk to each other by telephone at a moment's notice.

The concept of the market has undergone significant change in the

1990s. There has been a reinvention of the marketplace. Christopher Anderson, writing on the Internet, quotes one survey's findings. According to this survey, conducted in March 1998 by CommerceNet, an industry consortium, and Nielson, a media-research firm, 73 per cent of Internet users had used the Web for shopping in one way or another in the past month. Projections by International Data, a Massachusetts consultancy, show that by the

> *The Internet age offers the long-deferred promise of the sovereign consumer.*

year 2000, 46 million consumers in the US alone will be buying online, spending an average of $350 a year each. He cites Cisco Systems, a network-equipment maker, which is already selling products from its Web site at a rate of $1 billion a year. General Electric is saving a fortune by buying $1 billion worth of goods from its suppliers online. Dell Computer is selling $1 million worth of PCs a day on the Web.

Business Week in its 'Economic Viewpoint' section (19 January 1998) wrote that the Internet age offers the long-deferred promise of the sovereign consumer. All kinds of deals can now be found by surfing the Internet. A seller anywhere can find a willing buyer. The interaction of demand and supply takes place via the Internet. Barriers to competition will gradually disappear.

The economics of information – welcome back Adam Smith!

Experts say equal access to information for everyone will create the closest thing yet to Adam Smith's perfect market. For the past few years business transactions have been conducted by telephone and fax. Moving the process to the Internet makes it faster and easier. Many organizations are setting up Web sites to market their products and services.

Lorraine Harrington and Greg Reed (1996), say:

A new breed of intermediary is taking advantage of the economics of information. One of them may already be at work in your market, insinuated between you and your customers.

New entrants such as Industry.Net, IBEX, and Auto-By-Tel are using electronic networks to jump into the value chain in markets from software to industrial goods. The Internet's World Wide Web, along with the many private networks now emerging, allows these intermediaries to match buyers with sellers and deliver products and services at much lower cost and asset intensity than would be possible within a physical value chain.

Opportunities for buyers, sellers, and new intermediaries to create value in electronic channels are by no means limited to start-ups. Established companies are also moving to capitalize on the economic benefits and marketing reach of e-commerce technologies. Banks are moving to shift their customers to electronic channels – and cross-marketing related financial services such as brokerage and travel along the way. Retailers including Wal-mart and Kmart have announced on-line sales programmes. Some of these shifts are being driven by the entrance of new intermediaries; others are designed to discourage new entrants.

These moves indicate that electronic commerce – defined as the electronic exchange of information, goods, services and payments – has finally come of age.

Companies still mulling over technological issues – like how to establish a web site – and wondering when or if to include electronic commerce in their plans, may be missing opportunities or threats that are now emerging. Just about any industry is a fertile field for benefits to be captured or for new intermediaries to take hold. More than opportunity cost is involved for established players in such industries as financial services, electronics (including software), publishing, industrial goods, entertainment, healthcare, and retailing; electronic commerce holds the potential to place revenue stream at risk . . .

Electronic intermediation

This is really two separate opportunities: for an established player to reinvent its market, and for a new entrant to disintermediate existing relationships.

Asian industrial goods manufacturers exemplify the first kind of opportunity. Long active in export markets, and with a deep understanding of the economics of physical channels, they are now recognising the benefits of a virtual trading network that could reduce their selling and procurement costs quite significantly. Caught in the 1991–92 economic downturn in Japan, these manufacturers were searching for ways to stimulate sales in their home market. So they began buying up used machines and reselling them in the developing countries of Southeast Asia that could not yet afford new equipment. Buying and selling were conducted through a complex multi-tiered structure of brokers.

With the launch of a new virtual market, however, prospective buyers would be able, in return for an access fee, to log on and obtain basic make, model, and price information on machines offered by a range of manufacturers. They would be able to examine the title for authenticity to make sure they were not buying a stolen machine, and check the condition of the equipment by clicking on a series of close-up pictures . . .

For an illustration of the second type of opportunity for electronic intermediation, consider the potential of small, fast-moving companies like Industry.Net to shape markets by facilitating communications, negotiations, and eventually – when secure process software becomes available – transactions between sellers and buyers. Industry.Net is an electronic market place, originally specialising in high-tech manufacturing equipment but now offering the same menu of business-to-business communications and transactions support to a range of related product areas. Having begun as a business directory, it used the information it had built up about customers and suppliers to evolve into an electronic 'mall' providing electronic storefronts, product descriptions, job classifieds, directories and so on to over 4,500 members. With the potential to reduce participants' sales and marketing costs and also to extend their market reach, Industry.Net enables smaller companies to establish relationships with far-flung customers and suppliers that were previously outside their grasp.

Finally, commenting on reaching new segments and markets they write:

> Electronic channels offer companies the opportunity to gain incremental revenues by acquiring new customer segments or locking in current buyers. Wal-Mart's recent agreement with Microsoft, for example, is aimed at developing an on-line retailing service capable both of reaching potential customers who do not buy from their stores and getting deeper into the wallets of current consumers by providing them with a broader range of products.
>
> Wal-Mart is no stranger to using networks as a competitive advantage. By the early 1990s, it had already oriented its business around networks linking 20 to 30 automated distribution centres to 4,000 suppliers and some 2,400 stores. When the retail outlets began inputting product sales information automatically, the distribution centres were able to hold and ship goods more efficiently. As a result, Wal-Mart achieved much lower distribution costs than its competitors.
>
> *Source*: Reprinted with permission of the publisher from Lorraine Harrington and Greg Reed, 'Electronic commerce (finally) comes of age', *The McKinsey Quarterly*, 1996, No. 2, pp. 69–75. Copyright 1996 McKinsey & Company. All rights reserved.

Developments in electronic communication are thus going to transform the nature of the market and the way business transactions are conducted in practice. Information will be of vital importance in gaining and sustaining competitive advantage.

Electronic commerce in Europe

Philip Krauss (1998), partner of London solicitors, Church Adams Tatham, writes:

> Fears that European electronic commerce lacks a proper regulatory basis and will suffer by comparison with the US have led the European Commission to develop ambitious plans for harmonisation. By the end of the next decade a significant share of retail commerce is expected to be on the internet, putting pressure on regulators to provide easy and efficient means of payment.

Electronic commerce is a term whose usage varies according to context. It is not confined to the internet but includes other applications, such as videotex on which the French Mintel online information network is based.

Last year the Commission, which wants a framework for electronic commerce by 2000, identified four areas calling for a substantial contribution by regulators. They must:

● Devise a supervisory framework for the issue of electronic money.

● Provide guidance for issuers and users on transparency, liability and redress procedures.

● Clarify the application of the EU's competition rules to achieve a balance between interoperability and vigorous competition.

● Tackle the risk of fraud by improving security.

The author emphasizes the need for international practice. An established legal framework is vital if businesses are to have the confidence to make greater use of electronic commerce.

VERDICT

The market is constantly inventing itself and it will continue to do so as the globalization process accelerates and as technological developments bring into existence 'virtual' markets. Various authors have peppered their articles with examples to show how the simple concept of marketplace has been transformed into a concept of marketspace. The interaction of demand, supply and price have to be looked at from the point of view of these developments. Economics takes a very simplistic view of markets. As someone has said, economics strips markets of their complexity and variability, aggregating firms and individuals into two groups: buyers and sellers – demand and supply.

Access to information is eliminating imperfections in the marketplace thus bringing the economy closer to Adam Smith's perfect market.

MARKET FAILURES

Economists do recognize that there are some circumstances which lead to market failures, i.e. when the efficient allocation of scarce resources is hindered. Economists highlight the following circumstances of market failures:

- *Imperfect competition*: Where there are too many imperfections in the marketplace such as lack of knowledge on the part of buyers and sellers, differences in cost situations, barriers to entry and so on.
- *Externalities*: Factors such as traffic congestion, pollution and noise arise as side effects of production and consumption. Such by-products are not included in the demand–supply equilibrium scenario. Producers and buyers do not include the cost of pollution or congestion in their costs or prices.
- *Imperfect information*: In practice buyers and sellers do not have perfect information about the goods and services they buy and sell.
- *Strategic alliances and partnerships*: Alliances and partnerships take place in order to manipulate markets and prices. (This aspect will be dealt with in more detail in Gateway Four.)
- *Uncertainty*: Risks and uncertainty are part and parcel of doing business in a fiercely competitive environment.

Economists recognize that in practice there are a myriad of market failures. At macro level various governments have taken actions to minimize such market failures and to promote more competition in order to improve the performance of the market. Such actions include privatization, deregulation and competition policy which are based on the premise that more competition is better than less.

Paul A. Geroski (1997) defines market failure as:

   . . . the term economists reserve for situations where transaction costs become excessive. The result of market failure is that too few people participate in the market. At the extreme, when transaction costs become very large relative to the purchase price the market will cease to exist. In a sense transaction costs are like a sales tax and they can stunt the growth and development of a market in exactly the same way as excessive taxation.

The kind of markets that often operate poorly (if they operate at all) are those concerned with the production and sale of information, and the consequence of market failure is that too little investment in the provision of information is likely to be made by transacting agents.

Investments in R&D are a classic example of another type of activity, which, many people believe, is inhibited by excessive market failure. The problem arises because information is a public good. In the language of economists this means that information is both *non-rival* and *non-exclusive*.

Geroski cites the example of a good idea. It is difficult for anyone to establish property rights over particular ideas. As a result, it is very difficult for a seller of a good idea to realize its true value since ideas can be used again and again once acquired by buyers. Copyrights, intellectual property rights and patents are ways to protect property rights, but they introduce imperfections into the marketplace.

Due to the existence of many types of market failure in practice many companies form different types of alliance and partnership in order to manage markets and competition.

Market instability and lock-in

The three characteristics, namely cost advantage, network effects, and groove-in effects, according to Professor Brian Arthur of Santa Fe University, produce increasing returns and make markets very unstable. Network effects come into play when there is wide adoption of a specific product in the market. As more people use this product the likelihood of others also using it increases. Groove-in effects, on the other hand, mean that the more a specific product is used the more users become familiar and comfortable with that product. The users become reluctant to move to another product.

Instability of markets is explained by Professor Arthur in one of his replies in an interview with Joel Kurtzman (1998). He says:

> What am I saying is that under increasing returns, and under very specific mathematical conditions, markets become unstable. One product, one company, can take a great deal of the market, 70, 80, 90 per cent. Think of America On-line, think of Microsoft's dominance in computer operating systems, think of Intuit's Quicken, think of Java. And think of Boeing – it doesn't necessarily have to be in the computer industry.
>
> You get these dominances. In high tech, you see companies getting very wealthy, cash rich, buying other companies, merging and so on. You don't see this in steel and lumber and cement and dog chow and corn flakes. There may be large branded companies, but you don't see anything quite like high tech.
>
> So what am I saying here? I am saying that small events early on can get magnified by the force of increasing returns, as they might in presidential primaries. Under certain conditions, that can lock in the market to dominance of one product.
>
> Am I saying it's never the best product? No. I'm saying sometimes things go wrong and we lock into a cluster, like DOS, which computer people tell me was unimpressive. It locked in for 10 years even though there was a superior alternative on the market, the Macintosh operating system. It locked in because if everybody down the hall had DOS, I had to have DOS. It was safe to buy IBM because everybody was buying IBM . . . There tends to be an instability when a market is just starting out, say Java versus ActiveX. It's often difficult to say how things are going to go. But as one side gets farther ahead, gets more advantage and locks in the market, there is a period of stability. Then nothing much happens until the next wave of technology rolls over into something different. So these lock-ins are not for ever. Lotus 1-2-3 locks in spreadsheets for a while. Digital lock in minicomputers for 10 years. But then Digital is bypassed with workstations and PCs. That's certainly one reason why I'm not too concerned about lock-ins.

Source: Joel Kurtzman, 'Thought leader: W Brian Arthur', *Strategy & Business*, second quarter, 1998, p. 100. Copyright Booze Allen & Hamilton.

Professor Arthur highlights the relationship between increasing returns and instability of the markets. As the high-tech sector expands the economy will be dominated by 'lock-ins' due to the impact of increasing returns. He thus believes that far more attention should be paid to the concept of increasing returns than to the principle of diminishing returns.

VERDICT

Market imperfections are business reality. Market stability, instability, lock-ins and unlocking are the result of some companies, especially high-tech companies, building up market share and impacting the user base. It is important to get a realistic picture of what is going on in the economy.

EXECUTIVE SUMMARY

Competition

- Economics categorizes competition into perfect and imperfect competition. Within imperfect competition exist oligopoly, duopoly and monopoly.

- Competition exists as a result of various national and international factors. Professor Michael Porter of Harvard Business School highlighted five key forces contributing to a competitive environment: barriers to entry, availability of substitutes, bargaining power of buyers, bargaining power of suppliers and actions of rival competitors.

- Government policy, apart from constituting a barrier to entry for new entrants, has come up with privatization and deregulation which intensifies competition. Privatization in the UK is cited as an example to highlight the benefits of such a policy.

- Many countries are now riding a deregulation bandwagon to facilitate 'free' trade and promote competition. Such a policy reinforces the process of globalization.

- Competition is becoming increasingly intense. Companies cannot afford to be complacent. Okidata had to learn a hard lesson against the onslaught of Hewlett Packard.

- In the private sector many firms are formulating varying strategies to manage competition. One particular strategy is *time-pacing*, by which companies like Intel compete in the markets that won't stand still.

Markets

- A market in economics is defined as a place where buyers and sellers are brought together. Price mechanism brings buyers and sellers together and acts as an efficient distributor of scarce resources.

- The 1990s saw the transformation of the marketplace into marketspace as a result of the development of information technologies and electronic commerce.

- Electronic intermediation has brought about the reinvention of the market and created relationships among the various parties involved in specific transactions.

- The interaction of demand and supply and the new nature of the marketplace have to be viewed through an electronic lens.

- In practice there are many factors that lead to market failures. To cope with such market failures, companies enter into various forms of alliances and partnerships.

- Market failures, stability, instability, lock-ins and unlocking are the phenomena of modern business. Economists have to start paying attention to these phenomena and their causes.

References

Day, George and Reibsten, David (1997) 'Keeping ahead in the competitive game' in *FT Mastering Management*. London: Financial Times Management, 602.

Eisenhardt, Kathleen M. and Brown, Shona L. (1998) 'Time pacing: competing in markets that won't stand still', *Harvard Business Review*, March–April, 59–60.

Geroski, Paul A. (1997) 'Meaning of market failure' in *FT Mastering Management*. London: Financial Times Management, 468.

Goodman, John B. and Loveman, Garry W. (1991) 'Does privatisation serve the public interest?', *Harvard Business Review*, November–December, 28.

Harrington, Lorraine and Reed, Greg (1996) 'Electronic commerce (finally) comes of age', *The McKinsey Quarterly*, 2, 69–75.

Krauss, Philip (1998) 'Quest for card code', *Financial Times*, 24 February, 12.

Kurtzman, Joel (1998) 'Thought leader: W. Brian Arthur', *Strategy & Business*, second quarter, 100.

Miller, Alan M (1994) 'Privatisation: lessons from the British experience', *Long Range Planning*, 27 (6), 125–36.

Gateway Four

STRATEGIC ALLIANCES AND PARTNERSHIPS
Till death us do part!

When it comes to the tricky business of merging a successful group of companies, it is clear that two and two don't always make four.

Price Waterhouse

INTRODUCTION

M ergers, alliances and partnerships have dominated economic activities in the 1980s and 1990s. Most alliances have taken place in the name of efficiency and allegedly in the interests of consumers. In economics logical explanations are provided for mergers and alliances. But in reality is the picture different? Do alliances make business sense? Why do most of them fail? What are the key success factors that hold alliances together?

CONFIGURING COMPETITION – MARKET POWER VERSUS MARKET SIZE

According to economists, firms can grow by taking either the internal route (organic growth) or the external route. To develop internally would require investment in plant, technology and people and it takes time. If a company is doing well it will soon face the need to expand. There comes a time when buying, merging or forming an alliance becomes the most efficient, least expensive way to grow.

When mergers and acquisitions take place, new identities are created. In the case of alliances and strategic partnerships, the companies involved maintain their identities.

Integration of businesses is one of the avenues of growth advocated in economics. There are two types of integration – namely, vertical and horizontal. Vertical integration incorporates the production of raw materials and the manufacturing of finished products. An example of a fully integrated firm would be a rubber producing firm integrating with a tyre manufacturing firm which in turn is integrated with a tyre distribution outlet. In practice there are numerous examples of partial vertical integration, for example breweries taking over pubs or petrol companies taking over service stations. We now have Elf, Shell or BP service stations.

> *There comes a time when buying, merging or forming an alliance becomes the most efficient, least expensive way to grow.*

When a manufacturing firm integrates only with a supplier of raw materials it is known as backward vertical integration. When a manufacturing firm integrates only with a distribution outlet it is known as forward vertical integration.

Kimya M. Kamshad of the London Business School (1997) highlights the pros and cons of vertical integration.

Generally speaking, vertical integration is most attractive when different types of market failures exist that threaten profitability. Bringing production in-house allows a company to internalise and thereby overcome market failures. But the strategy is not without its own costs in terms of efficiency and price.

Vertical integration is often the best solution where the activity in question is complex and hard to define under conventional legal contracts. Thus there is a moral hazard problem involved with contracting out, if the contracting company cannot be legally covered for all possible contingencies . . .

Similarly, vertical integration will be attractive when outside suppliers of the activity are few and are likely to behave opportunistically, i.e. if there are not many suppliers then those that do exist may be able to exercise market power and extract economic rents in supplying the service in question. Such rent extraction by suppliers can be avoided if a company produces the activity in-house.

Horizontal integration involves the coming together of firms which are at the same level of production or are involved in similar processes. An example of horizontal integration would be when two clothing manufacturing firms integrate to share similar processes or to produce diversified products. When one bank merges with another bank the result is horizontal integration. In the 1960s the term 'conglomerate' became commonplace for integrated companies producing diversified products in order to minimize risks.

During the 1990s different types of strategic alliances and take-overs have become prominent features of international business. In the late 1980s and early 1990s take-over activity became very intense.

Examples of mergers and acquisitions in the 1980s

- Maxwell Communications Corporation took control of Macmillan by buying the US book publishers for £2.6 billion.
- ICI became Canada's biggest paint maker when the company paid $50 million to Sherwin Williams to gain control of their subsidiary BAPCO.
- Electrolux of Sweden became the number one global domestic appliance producer with its $745 million acquisition of White Consolidated Co.

> *During the 1990s different types of strategic alliances and take-overs have become prominent features of international business.*

- WPP of the UK transformed its operations and image by purchasing J. Walter Thompson. WPP was transformed into one of the world's leading marketing services company.
- Saatchi and Saatchi bought Ted Bates for $450 million to become the world's largest advertising agency.
- A merger between Smith Kline Beckman of the US and Beecham of the UK created a huge pharmaceutical group.
- Sony of Japan purchased CBS Records of the US for $2 billion.
- Sweden's Asea merged with Brown Boveri of Switzerland to form Asea Brown Boveri (ABB), the world's leading engineering company.
- In Spain the two largest domestic banks, Banco Central and

Banisto, merged after two regional banks, Banco Bilbao and Banco de Vizcaya, merged to create the country's second largest financial institution.

- Coopers & Lybrand merged with Deloitte Haskins and Sell to become a big consulting/auditing practice.

These examples of mergers and acquisitions show an extraordinary increase in take-over activity in the 1980s and this activity is showing no sign of abatement.

The 1980s was one of the most active decades for mergers and acquisitions in history. One economist commenting in June 1998 said that the mergers that looked like earthquakes in the 1980s will look like tremors by comparison with the 1990s.

The story in the 1990s

The 1990s is also a very active period for mergers, acquisitions and strategic alliances. According to Securities Data, in 1997 there were 6133 international deals worth $411 billion, compared to 3915 deals totalling $102 billion in 1992. The following are some of the highlights:

- in 1992 the Honk Kong and Shanghai Banking Corporation took over Midland Bank PLC; the result was the creation of the second largest non-Japanese bank in the world and the largest in the UK;
- a joint venture was set up between Krupp Hoesch and Thyssen (steel making) with Thyssen retaining 60:40 control;
- British Airport Authority (BAA) acquired 70 per cent of Gesac, the Italian company managing Naples airport;
- Guiness and Grand Metropolitan merged to create a drinks group called Diageo;
- the UK's ICI bought Anglo-Dutch Unilever's speciality chemicals businesses for $8 billion;

- the Italian phone company Stet bought 25 per cent of Mobilkom, Austria, 49 per cent of Telecom, Serbia, and 60 per cent of Retevision;
- the US Xerox Corporation (US) acquired the remaining 20% of Rank Xerox;
- Matsushita of Japan joined British Telecom, BSkyB and Midland Bank in a $41.1 billion joint venture to launch digital television in the UK;
- UK's Amersham International, in a $1.8 billion merger with Norwegian Nycomed, formed the world leader in diagnostic imaging agents;
- Lufthansa formed Star Alliance with SAS, United Airlines, Air Canada, and Thai Airways;
- Zurich Insurance merged with the financial services operations of the UK's BAT Industries;
- Anglo–Dutch publisher Reed Elsevier's $8.8 billion stock swap was agreed with German–Dutch rival Wolters Kluwer.
- in Switzerland, SBC and UBS joined in a $29 billion merger;
- US Merrill Lynch bought Mercury Asset Management for $5.3 billion;
- British Gas acquired a 61 per cent stake in India's Gujarat Gas Co.;
- General Electric Co. bought out its Indian partners' stakes in lighting and medical-equipment businesses;
- Industrial Credit & Investment Corp. of India acquired ITC Classic, the finance arm of tobacco-maker Indian Tobacco Co., a division of the UK's BAT Industries;
- Coopers & Lybrand merged with Price Waterhouse.

At the time of writing the following deals are being talked about:

- Compaq and Digital Equipment Corp concluded a $8.7 billion acquisition. The deal is said to be the largest in the annals of the computer industry. According to *Business Week* (9 February 1998), 'It will create a new computer colossus with some $37.5 billion in revenues, second only to giant IBM in computer sales.'

- The world's largest-ever merger between Citicorp and Travelers. The $70 billion deal will merge Citicorp and Travelers Group to create a megabank with global reach and nearly $700 billion in assets. The new company will be called Citigroup. Pundits have hailed this merger as the bank of the future.

- On Easter Monday 1998, a merger was announced between BankAmerica and NationsBank to create America's biggest bank. Both the Fed and the Justice Department cleared the deal.

- Worldcom's snatched MCI from the grasp of British Telecommunications for $37 billion.

- The $40 billion merger of Daimler-Benz and Chrysler. This deal will create the world's third largest auto company by revenue, fifth largest by sales.

- British Petroleum (BP) announced a £30.3 billion takeover of Amoco of the US. The deal will create the UK's largest company and a giant to rival Shell and Exxon.

Why do companies merge or form alliances?

Analysis of the reasons behind numerous acquisitions and strategic alliances highlights the following motives:

- to improve competitive positioning of the firm vis-à-vis rivals – strategic alliances are made to deter entry into the market;
- one partner may use an alliance as a means of acquiring a major new competence for its core business;
- to achieve sales objectives for export markets;
- to promote effective marketing through distributors;
- to create or build new businesses;
- to improve competitive position when neither partner is prepared to divest its operations completely;
- to achieve economies of scale and scope;

- to restructure an overcrowded business sector;
- to change corporate direction;
- to collaborate on research and development;
- to give businesses a global dimension;
- to become a key global player;
- to reduce the costs of new ventures, particularly high-tech new ventures;
- to overcome local market peculiarities;
- to achieve financial efficiency by taking over another firm in order to acquire undervalued assets;
- to survive in the marketplace. According to one German venture capitalist, 'Any company not now No. 1 or No. 2 in Europe in its particular market niche must either stand looking for prey to take over or become a target itself.'

According to Francis Bidault and Thomas Cummings (1997), both of IMD, alliances can bring the following hidden benefits:

- alliances can be a source of innovation – the factor influencing innovation is transfer of knowledge;
- alliances test processes in a new context – there is a potential for improvement in the way processes are managed;
- alliances can improve management processes;
- alliances can bring the challenge of competition to parts of an organization that are normally shielded from it.

VERDICT

Strategic alliances come into existence because (a) markets are becoming global, (b) the scale and scope of businesses is increasing, (c) product life cycles are becoming shorter, (d) there is a need for vast investment and (e) businesses operate in a turbulent marketplace.

STRATEGIC ALLIANCES AND INCREASING RETURNS

Alliances create integration of systems, structure, staff, products and processes. Combined competencies and knowledge deliver synergies and alliances and mergers lead to a situation of 2+2=5.

However, in practice success and synergies depend on meeting the needs of both organizations and people. Organizations have their own aspirations (What's in it for us?) as do employees (What's in it for me?).

What's in it for me? – examples of the corporate perspective

Asea Brown Boveri

ABB in the 1980s

In 1987 Sweden's Asea (founded in 1883) merged with Brown Boveri of Switzerland (founded in 1891) to form Asea Brown Boveri (ABB), the world's leading engineering company. The aim of Percy Barnavik, Chief Executive of ABB, was to turn ABB into the lowest cost producer in the world. He hoped to push changes that would achieve economies of scale and streamline manufacturing, marketing and financial operations. ABB has achieved considerable benefits from rationalization in a short timescale. In Europe ABB has become the biggest in the power equipment industry. In order to make further progress ABB made joint venture agreements with Westinghouse in the US and with Finmeccanica in Italy. The transmission and distribution agreement with Westinghouse added nearly $41.2 billion to ABB's turnover.

ABB hoped to generate 25 per cent of the group's turnover in the US by 1993. It forged ahead to acquire interests in different sectors in different parts of the world. Through BREL, British Rail's engineering subsidiary, bought in 1989 by a consortium in which ABB has a 40 per cent stake, ABB gained additional annual turnover of $450 million. ABB also has a share in Davis Coach and Locomotive Builder, a Swedish coach building concern, and a German high-speed train building company. The group had about 50 product-based business areas, some 800 companies and 3500 decentralized profit centres. ABB is a good example of how complex a merged group can become. The group consisted of 1000 companies and 36 business units which were organized into four business segments.

ABB in the 1990s

The group is still going strong and its chief executive officer until recently has featured in every management book as a leader who has effectively transformed the group. For the past seven years ABB's 'orders received' figures have been growing at 11 per cent compound rate and its pre-tax income during the same period has been growing at 21 per cent compound.

Its overall strategy throughout the 1990s has been to gain market share and to become cost efficient. ABB has 70 companies based in Central and Eastern Europe. Poland and the Czech Republic constitute a major platform for eastern expansion. ABB invest in emerging markets in order to establish market position in these regions and to maximize competitiveness by gaining local procurement, local engineering and local manufacturing.

Merger of Compaq and Digital Equipment

According to *Business Week* (February 1998):

> By acquiring Digital, Compaq is catapulted from the upstart, wild-and-woolly PC generation into the high tech big leagues of companies that supply the world's most complex and critical information systems. Compaq's product offering will now span the computing landscape, from $649 hand held computers to superpowerful $2 million fail-safe computer servers. More important the company will command Digital's vaunted

service and consulting staff of 22,000 people who know their way around the computing back offices of the world's largest corporations – customers Compaq has been striving to reach, with modest success, for the past three years.

Compaq is now able to cater for the full range of computer users at the top end of the computing market. The acquisition will deliver significant new revenues for Compaq.

The Citigroup megamerger

The purpose of the merger is to control more of consumers' finances by reaching a billion customers worldwide by 2010. Citigroup aims to become the biggest global financial service company by creating a financial supermarket.

According to *Business Week* (April 1998):

> Demographics are a key reason why this deal could work. The baby boomers of the US and Western Europe are entering their 50s – their peak saving years. That is opening up vast opportunities for all sorts of financial firms to sell investment-management services and products. For example, paced by inflows into retirement-savings plans, US mutual fund assets already total $4.8 trillion, and new money is coming in at a 30 per cent annual rate. Indeed a growing distrust of the world's retirement systems, many of them broke or nearly so, is boosting demand for mutual funds world-wide. So across Europe, Latin America, and even China, governments are beginning to set up privately funded retirement plans similar to the 401(k)s and IRAs of the US.

Citigroup, with the help of Travelers, will be able to extend its franchise in Latin America as far as private pension funds are concerned. The merger is also designed to minimize volatile earning streams and to facilitate the cross-selling of products.

BankAmerica and Nationbank merger

This merger was planned because of the need to find a partner to survive and to create a national brand in banking. By merging, the two banks expect to save $42 billion. The merger will consolidate their businesses and result in more effective use of market-tested skills of the two banks.

Mercedes-Benz and Chrysler

The merger between Mercedes-Benz and Chrysler will result in the following:

- Chrysler's reputation for quality will be enhanced;
- Mercedes can use Chrysler's US factory capacity to build more cars to meet demand;
- Chrysler's engineers can help build 'americanized' models;
- Mercedes can leverage Chrysler's know-how in sport utilities;
- it will provide a rich product mix;
- the enlarged company will become one of the top five revenue earning auto companies.

What's in it for me? – the people perspective

In many situations where alliances have failed researchers have found a culture clash and also unsatisfactory answers to the questions employees ask when their organizations merge. In practice, when employees join an organization they enter into a legal contract (employment contract) which indicates their terms of employment. Gradually, performance and psychological contracts come into existence. When companies merge, organizations have to consider the question: 'What's in it for the companies?' But employees on both sides have to ask a similar question:

> *When there is an overlap between organizational expectations and employees' expectations, there is a good chance of a merger or alliance succeeding.*

'What's in it for us?' When there is an overlap between organizational expectations and employees' expectations, there is a good chance of a merger or alliance succeeding (*see* Fig 4.1). One of the key success factors of alliances is a synergy between the corporate and people perspective.

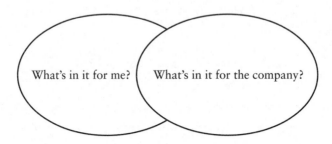

What's in it for me?   What's in it for the company?

Fig. 4.1 An overlap in expectations

DISECONOMIES OF MERGERS, ACQUISITIONS AND STRATEGIC ALLIANCES

In the late 1980s various studies were conducted to analyze why some mergers and alliances fail. The study, conducted by Harvard Business School under the leadership of Professor Michael Porter, found that successful acquirers in most cases diversify into related fields. Even successful diversifiers such as 3M and IBM had appalling records when they strayed into unrelated acquisitions. Diversifiers into unrelated fields, such as Cummins Engine, Gulf and Western, General Mills and Exxon, have had a remarkably poor take-over record. Harvard Business School used the disinvestment rate of earlier acquisitions as its prime measure of success and failure. By 1980 Cummins had divested all the unrelated acquisitions it had made since 1950, while Exxon and General Mills had each disposed of about 80 per cent of their unrewarding acquisitions.

McKinsey and Co. carried out a parallel study which examined the value creation performance of the acquisition programme of 116 large US and UK companies using financial measures. They came to similar conclusions to the Harvard study. The benchmark for success used by McKinsey was a company's ability at least to earn back its cost of capital on the funds invested in its acquisition programme.

> *Successful acquirers in most cases diversify into related fields.*

According to the McKinsey study, predators can make three cardinal errors which keep them from generating enough cashflow adequately to offset stock market acquisition premiums. They are:

- acquirers can overestimate the potential for synergy;
- market potential can be overestimated;
- integration after the take-over is badly handled.

The last factor is very important, especially in the light of megamergers taking place in the 1990s. In the merger of Citicorp and Travelers to form Citigroup, the two chief executives, John Reed and Sandy Weill, are going to share the top job. Many analysts predict that Citigroup will face integration problems and it is most likely that John Reed will be gone within a year. As far as the merger of NationBank and BankAmerica is concerned, it will be run by Hugh McCall Herad of Nationbank. However, management pundits predict difficulties of integration arising due to rival management teams.

The reason why the much applauded announcement of a merger between Glaxo Wellcome and SmithKline Beecham did not materialize was because the two chief executives, Richard Sykes of Glaxo Wellcome and Jan Leschly of SmithKline Beecham, did not see eye to eye on the issue of sharing the limelight. In giving evidence to the select committee, Jan Leschly indicated that he saw the proposed merger as a merger of equals, whereas Richard Sykes of Glaxo Wellcome, as it was alleged, wanted him to take a back seat.

Potential minefields

Sydney Finkelstein (1999) of Amos Tuck School of Business Administration highlights the potential minefields of cross-border mergers and acquisitions.

> Economists David J. Ravenscraft and William F. Long examined 89 acquisitions of US companies by foreign buyers between 1977 and 1990 and found that the operational performance of most of the buyers had not improved one year after the acquisition. Numerous anecdotal accounts corroborate these results.
>
> Take, for example, the acquisition of Columbia Pictures by Sony Corporation in 1989. After paying a significant premium for the company and keeping a hands-off attitude towards its senior executives in Hollywood, Sony was forced to accept an unprecedented $3.2 bn write-off in 1994.
>
> To understand why cross-border mergers and acquisitions are so difficult to implement, consider all that must go right in any (same-country) acquisition. The two companies must agree on:

- which products and services will be offered
- which facilities or groups will have primary responsibility for offering them
- who will be in charge of each of the facilities or groups
- where the expected cost savings will come from
- what the division of labour will look like in the executive suite
- what timetable will best generate the potential synergies of the deal.

These are the issues raised in relation to the mergers and acquisitions taking place within the same country. The problems are compounded when the mergers and acquisitions take place across borders. Differences in culture affects the way a company is managed, the way people within the organization are organized and managed, the way values and beliefs underpin behaviours and actions, and the way value is created for customers.

In the light of research undertaken by consultants and academics there are key factors that can be categorized as failure factors.

Why failures occur

Diseconomies and failures of mergers, acquisitions and other types of strategic alliance occur for the following reasons:

- too much attention is paid to the strategy of short-term profitability rather than long-term investment;
- there is a lack of strategic fit;
- it is often assumed that the skills in one business can readily be applied to another;
- many merged businesses have conflicting corporate cultures;
- there are differences in management styles and unclear business objectives;
- poor post-acquisition strategy is in place, and in some cases no such strategy is put in place
- some businesses see acquisitions as ends in themselves – acquisitions should be viewed as a strategy to reposition a business in a competitive environment;
- a common assumption is that the more closely related two companies are, the greater the economic benefits; the evidence, however, is inconclusive;
- the audit prior to acquisition has been incomplete;
- there is a failure to develop 'new' loyalties;
- the fascination of doing deals often leads to forgetting the reality of running a business – the implementation aspect is paid very little attention;
- too much time is spent finding and wooing a partner and little consideration is given to managing life after the union;
- what you see is not always what you get;
- an alliance will never be successful if you do not learn to trust your partner.

What makes acquisitions work?

The following are necessary if acquisitions are to succeed:

- clarity of purpose and objectives – a business strategy that makes sense
- good management in place at acquisition
- detailed advance planning
- a strategy of post-acquisition implementation
- thorough financial analysis
- previous experience with acquisitions
- attention to human resources
- continuous attention to communication
- recognition of the degree and level of dissimilarity.

The trick of success lies in how businesses are integrated when mergers and acquisitions take place. Sydney Finkelstein (1999) offers the following advice:

MANAGING THE INTEGRATION PROCESS

Given the importance of integration to acquisition success, how can companies best manage this process? There are several important considerations. Companies should:

Understand that most of the value creation in an acquisition occurs after the deal is done.

None of the synergies and benefits that are projected to accrue from an acquisition can be realised without substantial effort during the integration process.

Plan for integration before doing the deal.

There are many reasons why companies do not do this – such as time constraints, insufficient information and lack of awareness of how critical integration really is – but the alternative is essentially to guess at the sources of value creation. It is important to develop a checklist of key integration issues, assign personal responsibility and a timetable for dealing with these issues, and set targets that will help achieve the value creation needed to make the deal work.

Work out the details.

Some of the confusion and complexity of cross-border mergers can be mitigated by ensuring that early in the process, executives in an acquiring company learn about differences in accounting standards, labour laws, environmental regulations, and norms and regulations governing how business is conducted in the acquired firm's country.

Develop a clear communication plan and follow it throughout the entire process.

The prospective melding of different country cultures in a cross-border deal can easily compound the uncertainty employees experience in any merger and must be addressed in a proactive manner.

The success factors depend on the 'hard' issues as well as 'soft' issues such as communication and differences in national cultures. Economic rationality on its own is not enough.

The new game for the new economy

Professor Barry Nalebuff of Yale School of Management was speaking at a European Management Conference in April 1998 on the theme of 'co-opetition'. The book *Co-Opetition: Competitive and Cooperative Strategies for the Information Economy*, which he co-authored with Adam Brandenburger (1996) makes the point that the name of the game these days is to compete and collaborate with the same players. Professor Nalebuff suggests that so far the language of competition in business is a language of war (making a killing, beating the competitors, locking in suppliers, win–lose or win–win situation). What is increasingly happening is that the language of competition is

> *The name of the game these days is to compete and collaborate with the same players.*

being transformed into a language of peace. Co-operation is taking place to create value, rather than competition which captures value. The business game is changing. Companies like Intel, Microsoft, and Gap actively shape the game they play. According to Professor Nalebuff:

> The economy is dynamic and evolving. The players create new markets and take on multiple roles. They innovate. If this sounds like the free-form and rapidly transforming marketplace, that's why game theory may be the kernel of new economics for the new economy.

Garry Hamel, Yves L. Doz and C. K. Prahalad (1989) write:

> Collaboration between competitors is in fashion. General Motors and Toyota assemble automobiles, Siemens and Philips develop semiconductors, Canon supplies photocopiers to Kodak, France's Thomson and Japan's JVC manufacture videocassette recorders. But the spread of what we call 'competitive collaboration' – joint ventures, outsourcing agreements, product licensing, co-operative research – has triggered unease about the long-term consequences. A strategic alliance can strengthen both companies against outsiders even as it weakens one partner vis-à-vis the other. In particular, alliances between Asian companies and Western partners. Co-operation becomes a low cost route for new competitors to gain technology and market access.
>
> Yet the case for collaboration is stronger than ever. It takes so much money to develop new products and to penetrate new markets that few companies can go it alone in every situation. ICL, the British computer company, could not have developed its current generation and mainframes without Fujitsu. Motorola needs Toshiba's distribution capacity to break into the Japanese semiconductor market. Time is another critical factor. Alliances can provide shortcuts for Western companies and quality control.
>
> Companies that benefit most from competitive collaboration adhere to a set of simple but powerful principles.
>
> *Collaboration is competition in a different form.* Successful companies never forget that their new partners may be out to disarm them. They

enter alliances with clear strategic objectives, and they also understand how their partners' objectives will affect their success.

Harmony is not the most important measure of success. Indeed, occasional conflict may be the best evidence of mutually beneficial collaboration. Few alliances remain win–win undertakings forever. A partner may be content even as it unknowingly surrenders core skills.

Co-operation has limits. Companies must defend against competitive compromise. A strategic alliance is a constantly evolving bargain whose real terms go beyond the legal agreement or the aims of top management. What information gets traded is determined day to day, often by engineers and operating managers. Successful companies inform employees at all levels about what skills and technologies are off-limits to the partner and monitor what the partner requests and receives.

Learning from partners is paramount. Successful companies view each alliance as a window on their partners' broad capabilities. They use the alliance to build skills in areas outside the formal agreement and systematically diffuse new knowledge throughout their organisation.

Why collaborate?

Using an alliance with a competitor to acquire new technologies or skills is not obvious. It reflects new commitment and a capacity of each partner to absorb the skills of the other. We found that in every case in which a Japanese company emerged from an alliance stronger than its Western partner, the Japanese company had made a greater effort to learn.

Strategic intent is an essential ingredient in the commitment to learning. The willingness of Asian companies to enter alliances represents a change in competitive tactics, not competitive goals. NEC, for example, has used a series of collaborative ventures to enhance its technology and product competences. NEC is the only company in the world with a leading position in telecommunications, computers, and semiconductors – despite investing less in R&D (as a percentage of revenues) than its competitors like Texas Instruments, Northern Telecom, and L.M. Ericsson. A string of partnerships, most notably with Honeywell, allowed NEC to leverage its in-house R&D over the last two decades.

Western companies, on the other hand, often enter alliances to avoid investments. They are more interested in reducing the costs and risks of entering new businesses or markets than in acquiring new skills. A senior US manager often offered this analysis of his company's venture with a Japanese rival: 'We complement each other well – our distribution capability and their manufacturing skill. I see no reason to invest upstream if we can find a secure source of product. This is a comfortable relationship for us.'

An executive from this company's Japanese partner offered a different perspective: 'When it is necessary to collaborate, I go to my employees and say, "This is bad, I wish we had these skills ourselves. Collaboration is second best. But I will feel worse if after four year we do not know how to do what our partner knows how to do." We must digest their skills.'

The problem here is not that the US company wants to share investment risk (its Japanese partner does too) but that the US company has no ambition beyond avoidance. When the commitment to learning is so one-sided, collaboration invariably leads to competitive compromise.

. . . There are certain conditions under which mutual gain is possible, at least for a time:

> **The motives for collaboration include gaining time, gaining knowledge, enhancing skills and minimizing risk and cost.**

The partners' strategic goals converge while their competitive goals diverge. That is, each partner allows for the other's continued prosperity in the shared business. Philips and Du Pont collaborate to develop and manufacture compact discs, but neither side invades the other's market. There is a clear upstream/downstream division of effort.

The size and market power of both partners is modest compared with industry leaders. This forces each side to accept that mutual dependence may have to continue for many years. Long-term collaboration may be so critical to both partners that neither will risk antagonising the other by an overtly competitive bid to appropriate skills or competencies. Fujitsu's 1 to 5 size disadvantage with IBM means it will be a long time, if ever, before Fujitsu can break away from its foreign partners and go it alone.

Each partner believes it can learn from the other and at the same time limit access to proprietary skills. JVC and Thomson, both of whom make VCRs, know that they are trading skills. But the two companies are looking for very different things. Thomson needs product technology and manufacturing prowess; JVC needs to learn how to succeed in the fragmented European market. Both sides believe there is an equitable chance to gain.

Source: Reprinted by permission of *Harvard Business Review*. From Gary Hamel, Yves L. Doz, and C. K. Prahalad, 'Collaborate with your competitors – and win', *Harvard Business Review*, January–February, 1989, pp. 133–135. Copyright 1989 by the President and Fellows of Harvard College; all rights reserved.

The above article clearly illustrates the point that collaboration does not exclude competition. The motives for collaboration include gaining time, gaining knowledge, enhancing skills and minimizing risk and cost. The concept of collaboration is not the same as the concept of collusion in economics. Collaborating to compete is one of the new ways of doing business and it should be incorporated when considering the behaviour of the firm in economics.

DIVESTITURES

There are a number of options open to a divesting company when businesses have become peripheral or difficult to manage. Divestment may take the form of selling the business as a going concern, closing or spinning off. Philips, the Dutch electronics group, spun off its telecommunications and white goods businesses in joint ventures with US partners. ICI spun off its chemical business, Zeneca, as an independent company. Boots sometime ago sold three subsidiaries, Clement Clark International, Clement Clark and John Weis & Son, because it was believed that these activities did not meet the 'strategic fit' of Boots.

Businesses divest for the following reasons:

- to concentrate on their 'core' business activities
- to release resources or growth
- to restructure their corporate portfolio
- to get rid of problem companies
- to strengthen the balance sheet
- to enhance their strategic fit.

Divestiture is not an indication of failure or incompetent management. It is as important as acquisition to a company's strategic positioning.

VERDICT

Strategic alliances and partnerships are increasing in the late 1990s. Alliances take place for a variety of reasons but they also have disadvantages (diseconomies). Many experts now argue that to gain and sustain competitive advantages, companies not only have to play competitive games but they have to form alliances to create new rules to suit their strategies.

Many megamergers in the financial, pharmaceutical and auto sectors will enable companies to position themselves for the new millennium.

CONTROL OF MERGERS AND ACQUISITIONS – CREATION OF SURROGATE 'FREE' MARKETS!

Many countries have competition policies. This is a distinct form of regulation which tries to move markets to the perfectly competitive ideal. All countries have policies to regulate competition in order to safeguard consumers' interest.

In the UK the Monopolies and Restrictive Practices Commission was established in 1949 under the Monopolies and Restrictive

Practices (Inquiry and Control) Act, 1948. The Monopolies Commission was reconstituted under the Restrictive Trade Practices Act, 1956 and its functions were further extended by the Monopolies and Mergers Act, 1965.

The term 'monopoly' is interpreted by the Commission to indicate the existence of conditions where one supplier or a group of inter-connected bodies corporate, or a number of concerns which act in concert to restrict competition, control at least one third of the supply of specified goods and services. The Commission cannot itself initiate an inquiry. It inquires only into matters referred to it. In 1973 the Commission was renamed the Monopolies and Mergers Commission (MMC). A company can be referred if it supplies more than 25 per cent of the total market. There is no presumption that a monopoly is necessarily bad. Each case referred is considered on its own merit.

The Office of Fair Trading vets a proposed merger bid and advises the Secretary of State for Trade and Industry who then decides whether the bid should be referred to the Monopolies and Mergers Commission. The main consideration in the decision whether to refer a bid to the Monopolies and Mergers Commission is the potential effect on competition in the UK. For example, in the case of Nestlé's £2.1 billion bid for Rowntree, Lord Young, the then Trade and Industry Secretary, decided not to refer the bid to the Monopolies and Mergers Commission. He said, 'In deciding whether to refer a bid we look mainly at the effect on competition in the UK.' It was felt that Nestlé had only 2 per cent of the UK's chocolate market. If Nestlé merged with Rowntree then it would still be smaller than Cadbury. Nestlé combined with Rowntree would have 26 per cent of the chocolate market whereas Cadbury-Schweppes had 27 per cent of the market.

In the US, antitrust policy is responsible for monitoring market influence. Antitrust policies attack anticompetitive abuses by prohibiting certain kinds of business conduct and by restricting some market structures such as monopolies. The Department of Justice is the competent authority for enforcement of US anti-trust laws with respect to alliances.

The philosophy of the antitrust legislation in the US has shifted over the years from the attitude that big was bad to the attitude that big was not necessarily bad. What mattered was economic efficiency.

Control in the European Union

In the European Union the competition policy is designed to achieve three broad objectives:

- to prevent the erection of trade barriers consisting of restrictive agreements between undertakings, abuse of monopoly power or state subsidies
- to preserve effective competition as a foundation for the creation of the Single Market
- to encourage efficiency, innovation and lower prices.

Merger control regulation

Merger Control Regulation relates to the control of concentrations between undertakings. A concentration is defined as the merger of two or more previously independent undertakings or the acquisition of direct or indirect control of all or part of one or more undertakings by persons controlling undertakings or by undertakings themselves.

If a concentration with a EU dimension creates or strengthens a dominant position as a result of which effective competition would be significantly impeded, the Commission must declare the concentration to be incompatible with the Single Market and, therefore, prohibited.

Article 85 of the European Community Treaty prohibits restrictive agreements which have as their object or effect the prevention, restriction or distortion of competition within the Community.

The Commission treats it as axiomatic that where there is an agreement to establish a joint venture between actual or potential competitors, that agreement has inherent anti-competitive effects and therefore falls within Article 85. Whether or not the joint ventures are actual or potential, competitors are assessed from the supply side, rather than from the demand side.

Article 86 of the Treaty relates to abuse of a dominant position. The primary test used to determine whether or not an undertaking enjoys a dominant position, i.e. the power to act independently disregarding its competitors, is to look at that undertaking's share of the relevant market. When a market share of the allegedly dominant undertaking is in itself insufficient to establish the existence of the dominant position, the Commission may consider other facts such as strong vertical integration, a technology lead over its competitors, a strong brand name, strict quality control, a highly developed sales network, a wide range of products, ownership of critical industrial property rights and a mature market.

Competition policies in Europe and the US are designed to promote competition by reducing imperfections in the market. The object is to take an undertaking as near to 'perfect competition' behaviour as possible.

Some economists argue that competition laws are necessary in order to maintain an entrepreneurial culture. Such laws are branded as 'the Magna Carta of free enterprise'. As one commentator has said: 'Markets are sublime institutions, but they require a referee.'

The trust busters – some examples

The alliance IPSP is a venture comprising a satellite operating company (Orion), satellite manufacturers (BAe and matra-Hachette), carriers (Kingston Communications and STET) and an industry investor (Nissho Ewai). The business of the venture was to provide private international business telecommunications services and bulk satellite capacity. The Commission gave a negative clearance on the grounds that the market was dominated by the public telecommunications operators and their alliances so that there were strong barriers to entry with few private initiatives in this sector.

In Holland Media Group – a joint venture between RTL, a Luxembourg broadcasting group (contributing two Dutch commercial TV channels) Veronica (owner of a third Dutch channel), and Endemol (largest independent producer of TV programmes in the Netherlands) – was refused clearance by the Commission because the venture would create a dominant position on the Dutch TV advertising market and strengthen Endemol's existing dominant position in the Dutch TV production market.

A proposed alliance between British Airways and American Airlines has been under consideration by the Commission since October 1996 (*see* below). The alliance awaits approval in the US. European Union Commissioner Van Miert wants British Airways to give up some of its take off and landing slots free to its competitors. British Airways wants to sell these slots – about 267 of them at Heathrow and Gatwick – for £2 million a piece. Peter Mandelson, Trade Secretary, and Neil Kinnock, the European Union Transport Commissioner, appear to support British Airways.

In the US the Justice Department disallowed Microsoft's proposed acquisition of Intuit, the maker of Quicken, an accounting and financial software package.

The Federal Trade Commission blocked McKesson's purchase of Amerisource Health and Cardinal Health's take-over of Bergen Brunswick in the interests of preserving competition in drug wholesaling.

The European Commission asked Boeing Co. to renegotiate its take-over of McDonnell Douglas Corp. in order to mimimize the impact of its market share and coverage.

US versus Europe

In the editorial column of the *Financial Times* (1998) it was stated:

> Brussels is examining a range of alliances, including the proposed link-up between British Airways and American Airlines and the partnership between United Airlines of the US and Lufthansa of Germany. The US has to make up its mind about BA–American, but the United–Lufthansa alliance is already functioning because Washington has given it immunity from the anti-trust laws.
>
> Washington and Brussels differ on two issues. First, Mr. Hunnicutt says Mr. van Miert is paying too much attention to individual routes, such as Frankfurt to New York, and too little to the effect of alliances on the transatlantic market. While airline partners can reduce competition on the few routes on which they both fly, he argues, alliances can have a beneficial effect on competition overall. This is because they use their combined networks to offer flights to many more destinations, thereby increasing competition between alliances.
>
> The second difference is over how regulators should reduce the power of alliances on routes where they are too powerful. Washington relies on 'carve outs', which means alliances are denied anti-trust immunity on those routes. Instead of offering uniform fares, they have to provide competing service and prices. Mr. van Miert's remedy is to reduce the number of flights alliance partners are allowed to offer on routes they both serve, thereby encouraging other airlines to set up competitive services. Mr. Hunnicutt argues, this could lower the number of seats available, pushing up prices. It is an important argument because the trend towards concentration in the industry is accelerating. As well as the transatlantic alliances, US airlines, such as United and Delta, have been forming domestic partnerships.

Free competition and the Microsoft dilemma

In 1995 the Justice Department charged Microsoft with using its near-monopoly of operating systems to stifle competitors. Microsoft

signed a consent agreement promising to avoid anti-competitive practices. In December 1997 Microsoft were given a warning about
anti-competitive practice.

According to an article in *Business Week* (1998):

America's high-tech industry is the economic success story of the 1990s.
Accounting for some 30% of the increase in gross domestic product since
1994, the explosive growth of the country's software and computer companies has enabled the US to regain its supremacy in the global
marketplace. Not since the heyday of the railroads in the 1800s has prosperity been tied so closely to one sector of the economy.

The engine inside this economic steamroller is Microsoft Corp., which
provides the operating system for virtually all personal computers, along
with the leading applications and many of the top programming tools.
With a single company setting key software standards, businesses and
consumers are able to buy software and hardware without worrying
about compatibility. And the computer industry has mushroomed into a
$700 billion business.

But few have grown as much as Microsoft. In 1997, Microsoft's $3.4
billion in net income accounted for 41% of the profits of the 10 largest
publicly traded software companies, by *Business Week's* calculation. Now,
Microsoft, with its $10 billion cash pile and 25,700 employees, is reaching
beyond the PC into new markets – everything from computerised toys and
TV set-top boxes to selling cars and airline tickets over the Internet.

The sheer pervasiveness of Microsoft in an increasingly digital world
raises profound questions: Should a single company exercise so much economic power? And what should the government do, if anything?

These may well be the most critical economic-policy decisions facing
the US today. And they are coming to a head later this month (April,
1998). Microsoft is expected to launch its publicity blitz for Windows
98 – a new version of its operating system. This product release is light-
ning rod from an antitrust viewpoint, since it integrates an Internet
browser, a new product, into Windows – an existing monopoly. Any
day now, the Justice Department is expected to force Microsoft to provide
an alternative version of Windows without the browser.

In May 1998, Microsoft and the US Justice Department appear to be heading for the most contentious and costly anti-trust battle in decades. This dispute is expected to last for a very long time.

It is asserted that Microsoft has illegally used its *market power* to stifle competition in other parts of the computer industry, employing predatory pricing policies and contract restrictions. Microsoft want computer manufacturers

> *Should Microsoft be left alone to continue to innovate?*

to take its Internet Explorer browser. It is a condition of licensing Windows 95. This created a market disadvantage for Netscape, the company's main competitor in the browser market. In its new version of Windows 98 Microsoft has included its own browser free of charge.

Questions and considerations

The questions are: Should Microsoft be left alone to continue to innovate? Should Microsoft be broken up into different companies? Should trust busters regulate Microsoft's business practices? Does Microsoft's dominant position harm the economy? Are consumers benefiting from Microsoft's dominant position? Has Microsoft, the world's third largest company by market value, become a monopolistic menace in an arena where technologies relating to telecommunications, computers and media are converging? Would regulating Microsoft stifle innovation?

These are fundamental questions which economists have to address in regulating competition. The dynamics of competition are changing constantly. We may have many Microsofts in the future configuring the competitive climate. The regulatory system has to consider such developments and adjust to the changing times ahead.

Professor Arthur of Santa Fe argues that trust busters have to be careful in controlling some high-tech companies which gain dominance due to increasing returns. Controlling such companies will kill innovation. Again, quoting from the interview he gave (Kurtzman, 1998), he says:

> People innovate and innovate and innovate in high tech. They are ready-ing these products, they're getting them going with the knowledge that if they lock in the market, they're going to get very rich and if they don't, they're going to lose everything. So they are making large bets.
>
> That makes high tech a very different culture. It becomes mission-oriented. It's always looking for the next big thing. It makes it more like a casino.
>
> Another metaphor I use is that it is like a land rush of the 1880s. Companies are all behind a starting line and whoever takes that market first, gets it. I don't think that we should worry about that, because that's the prize. It's not so much for risk taking as for innovation.
>
> But there's a big 'however'. If you have won six rushes in a row, that shouldn't mean that you can parlay your winnings into a four-wheel-drive instead of a horse. It also shouldn't mean that you're allowed to hobble the other horses in the dark.
>
> So I am in favour of free markets, but I'm in favour of fairness, too.

Source: Joel Kurtzman, 'Thought leader: W Brian Arthur', *Strategy & Business*, second quarter, 1998, pp. 100–101. Copyright Booze Allen & Hamilton.

Should market rules or legal rules drive competition?

Professor Ralf Boscheck (1995) of IMD, Lausanne, says current tech-nological and competitive forces cause a growing number of firms to leverage their skills and assets across wider markets:

> In the process the traditional view of firms, competing in clearly defined arenas, will be replaced by a broader notion of vertically and horizontally related activities whose co-ordination involves a mix of competition and co-operation, within and outside traditional market relations.
>
> Introducing an entirely new product concept, involving unique inputs, processes, and channels of distribution, may at the outset require broadly integrated operations simply because the needed ingredients are not

widely available, or the initial volume does not justify any productive spe-cialisation other than through the entrepreneurial innovator himself. Hence, to the extent that the typical venture initially needs to take over all, or most, of the vertically related activities, it develops and nurtures those assets and skills required to operate the entire industry on a limited product and geographic scope. The situation changes, once a growing market volume allows for some degree of specialisation. Selective deinte-gration sets in, and companies focus on developing their skill-base in support of expanding technology applications, product-lines and geo-graphic market. As markets mature, the continuation of the selective deintegration results in companies leveraging their control over vital tech-nologies, assets and skills through a network of co-ordinating relations across broadest geographic and product markets, product line exten-sions, as well as emerging product areas. Obviously, all three types of company organisations can coexist in the ultimate phase. Yet, from an efficiency point of view, overly integrated operations under one owner-ship run the risk of bureaucratic degradation where markets support a larger degree of productive specialisation among independently owned operations linked through efficient market contracts, i.e. price and/or commercial arrangements. Obviously also, industries differ with regard to the extent and timing of these organisational patterns. In general, how-ever, an acceleration sets in. Once the required level of fixed costs per activity is lowered, the general market volume increases, and the cost of stipulating, monitoring and enforcing market contracts can be reduced. Whereas the former two drivers depend on basic technological change and the extent of the market that can be reached, the latter depends to a significant extent on the perspective of competition policy authorities vis-à-vis contractual and tacit commercial arrangements.

Evidently, current market realities limit the regulator's ability to type-cast competitive behaviours for the purpose of rule making and law enforcement. Already hard pressed to define the market boundaries and the economic impact of competitive actions under conventional market conditions – the question is how to create legal certainty for – rather than prohibiting – new forms of company organizations and industrial structures.

Contrary to the current legislative trend, not broad regulations but case-based evaluations of specific commercial relations and industrial structures would be required to assure legal justice and economic efficiency. The basic adequacy of numerous competition and enforcement mechanisms – laying out the context in which companies are permitted to shape and adjust to their evolving competitive environment – needs to be reassessed. Should market rules or legal rules drive competition? What are the implications for companies today?

Source: Reprinted from *Perspectives for Managers*. With permission from IMD.

In regulating competition, 'trust busters' have to take into consideration economic as well as non-economic factors. The market is now dominated by different types of industrial structure. One has to examine these individually and consider their implications with reference to consumer benefits.

VERDICT

Trust busters are necessary to protect consumer interest and control the market power of monopolies rather than the market size. However, the legislation in many countries is not geared to controlling strategic alliances and partnerships. The merger authorities also have to strike a balance between temporary monopolies due to market lock-in and other types of monopolies and use their discretion to assess business situations and control market power.

EXECUTIVE SUMMARY

- **In economics mergers and acquisitions are treated under the theme of integration. Very little attention has been paid to strategic alliances and partnerships which have become the key features of today's industrial structure.**

- Integration is categorized as vertical or horizontal. Both types constitute avenues for business growth.

- Vertical integration in practice becomes very attractive when different types of market failure exist that threaten profitability.

- Since 1980 different types of strategic alliances and partnerships have come into existence. At the same time during this period, and more so now, we see the development of megamergers in different industrial sectors.

- Currently 'the talk of the town' is the mergers between Citicorp and Travelers, BankAmerica and NationalBank, and Daimler-Benz and Chrysler.

- Companies merge to gain advantages relating to technology, market positioning and learning new skills in a short time. Various cases illustrate the response to the question 'what's in it for me?'

- Beside mergers and acquisitions, consideration has to be given to various types of strategic alliance. In the fast growing market successful strategic alliances depend on increasing returns, destabilizing market values, a chain of timely ideas and key dimensions of competition.

- Many writers omit 'people issues' when dealing with mergers and acquisitions or strategic alliances. The people issue constitutes one of the key factors on which the success of various ventures depends.

- Not all alliances are good news. Many factors contribute to what the economists would term 'diseconomies'.

- To make alliances and acquisitions work, attention has to be paid to strategy, structure, technology and people.

- Management 'experts' like Hamel, Prahalad, Doz and now Nelbuff argue the case for collaborating to win. Increasingly we will witness competitors collaborating in order to gain and sustain competitive advantage.

- Apart from mergers and acquisitions and various forms of strategic alliance, many organizations which have merged are also divesting their businesses in order to 'stick to their knitting'.

- It is believed that mergers and acquisitions do not always lead to benefits for customers. For this reason many countries have measures to control such ventures.

- Trust busters constantly monitor business practices that lead to consumer exploitation and economic inefficiency.

- The dilemma facing many regulators are the developments taking place in the current competitive climate incorporating mega-mergers, market lock-ins due to increasing returns, and business practices adopted by such companies as Microsoft and Intel.

References

'Aviation Alliances', editorial column of the *Financial Times*, 5 May 1998.

Bidault, Francis and Cummings, Thomas (1997) 'Alliances can bring hidden benefits'in *FT Mastering Management*. London: Financial Times Management, 607–8.

Boscheck, Ralf (1995) 'Playing By Market Rules', *Perspectives for Managers*, 8 September, 2–4.

Cortese, A., France, M., Garland, S., Hamm, S. and Mandel, M.J. (1998) 'What to do about Microsoft', *Business Week*, 20 April, 43–53.

Finkelstein, Sydney (1999) 'Safe ways to cross the merger minefield' in *FT Mastering Global Business*. London: Financial Times Management, 119–23.

Glassgall, William (1998) 'Citigroup: Just the start', *Business Week* 20 April, 35.

Hamel, Gary, Doz, Yves L. and Prahalad, C.K. (1989) 'Collaborate with your competitors – and win', *Harvard Business Review*, January–February, 133–5.

Kamshad, Kimya (1997) 'Pros and cons of vertical integration' in *FT Mastering Management*. London: Financial Times Management, 471.

Kurtzman, Joel (1998) 'Thought leader: W. Brian Arthur', Strategy & Business, second quarter, 100–1.

Nalebuff, Barry and Brandenburger, Adam (1996) *Co-Opetition: Competitive and Co-operative Strategies for the Information Economy*. USA: Currency/Doubleday.

Williams, G., Sager, I., Judge, P.C. and Burrows P. (1998) 'Power Play', *Business Week*, 9 February, 35.

Gateway Five

BUSINESS ORGANIZATION

Making it focused, fast and flexible

Economists do not want to disturb the crystalline elegance of the neo-classical theory of the firm.

Jack Downie (1958)

INTRODUCTION

Marginal costing, profit maximization and a firm's equilibrium position play an important part in the economics of organizations. Have these concepts become redundant in the light of the growing importance of increasing returns?

Is the idea of the 'equilibrium position of a firm' any longer viable in a turbulent business climate?

What approaches and strategies do organizations need to adopt in order to manage complexity?

The bottom-line of any organization now is to become fast, flexible and focused.

THE THEORY OF THE FIRM

In economics the behaviour of business organizations is dealt with under *the theory of the firm*. What to produce, for whom to produce it and how much to produce depend on the cost of production and the price suppliers can charge to make a profit. Suppliers have to buy raw materials, manufacture and sell the products, either directly or through distributors and dealers.

Profit is the measure of a firm's success. Focus on profit led to focus on cost and in particular marginal cost. Costs are divided into average and marginal costs. The concept of marginal cost is very important and underpins the theory of the firm. *Marginal cost, together with marginal revenue, determines the level of output, price and profit.*

Let us take as an example a firm in the book publishing business. Its core business is to publish and sell textbooks. The cost structure of the firm in question is shown in Fig. 5.1.

Quantity (units)	Total cost (£s)	Average cost (£s)	Marginal cost (£s)
100	1000	10	10
200	2400	12	14
300	4500	15	21
400	7200	18	27

Fig. 5.1

Average cost is total cost/total units produced and marginal cost is the cost of producing an additional output.

Ideally a firm's average and marginal costs in the initial stage of production fall and then after a certain point diminishing returns set in and they begin to rise. When average costs (AC) increase, marginal costs (MC) will increase as well but faster than the average costs. Similarly when average costs fall, marginal costs will fall as well but faster than the average costs (*see* Fig. 5.2).

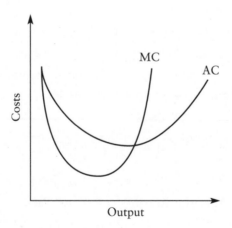

Fig. 5.2

Revenues of the firm

The revenues earned will depend on the price charged which, in turn, will depend on the market conditions a firm is operating in. A firm operating in a perfectly competitive market will be a price-taker. It cannot fix the price it wants to charge by manipulating supply. Its revenue position will be as shown in Fig. 5.3.

Quantity sold	Price/unit (£s)	Total revenue (£s)	Average revenue (£s)	Marginal revenue (£s)
10	5	50	5	5
20	5	100	5	5
30	5	150	5	5
40	5	200	5	5

Fig. 5.3

Average revenue is total revenue/quantity sold and marginal revenue is the additional revenue gained by selling an additional unit. In a perfectly competitive market a firm's average and marginal revenue will be the same.

If a firm is operating in an imperfectly competitive situation then its revenue situation will be as shown in Fig. 5.4.

Quantity sold	Price/unit* (£s)	Total revenue (£s)	Average revenue (£s)	Marginal revenue (£s)
10	5	50	5	5
20	4.5	90	4.5	4
30	4	120	4	3
40	3.5	140	3.5	2

Fig. 5.4

*The firm has to reduce its price in order to attract customers from its competitors. Both average revenue (AR) and marginal revenue (MR) will fall (*see* Fig. 5.5).

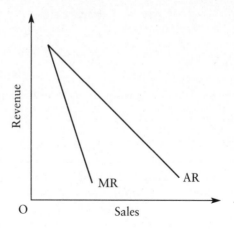

Fig. 5.5

The steepness of the average and marginal revenue curves will depend on the intensity of imperfect competition. A monopoly firm's average and marginal revenue curves will be much steeper than that of a firm operating in an oligopolistic or imperfectly competitive market.

Profit maximization and a firm's equilibrium

The theory of the firm assumes that all firms are in business to *maximize* profit. This is the main strategic objective. In order to maximize profit, irrespective of the market situations they are operating in, marginal revenue must equal marginal cost.

> *The theory of the firm assumes that all firms are in business to maximize profit.*

The profit of a firm in a perfect competition is maximized at price P_1 and quantity Q_1 (*see* Fig. 5.6). The profit of a firm in an imperfect competition is maximized at price P_2 and quantity Q_2 (*see* Fig. 5.7).

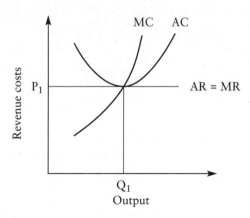

Fig. 5.6 A firm in a perfect competition

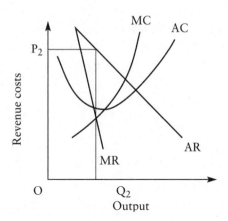

Fig. 5.7 A firm in an imperfect competition

In a monopoly situation, average and marginal cost curves will be relatively steep. The price charged will be higher and output sold will be less than in a firm in an imperfect competition (*see* Fig. 5.8).

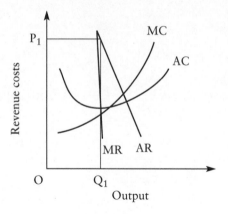

Fig. 5.8 A firm in a monopoly situation

The following are the assumptions behind the theory of the firm:

- the owner of the individual firm (entrepreneur) behaves rationally – this implies that the individual producer aims at earning the greatest possible money profits;
- entrepreneurs always produce each output as cheaply as possible given the prevailing technical conditions;
- the price of each factor of production is given and fixed;
- all units of each factor of production are equally efficient;
- there is an infinitely elastic supply of all the factors of production at their current price.

All firms will maximize profit when their marginal costs equal marginal revenues. The firms will be in equilibrium status.

Reality test

How realistic is the theory of the firm and how can it be transformed to fit the global economy within which large and small enterprises operate? As one economist has put it: 'The theory of competition is at once the pride and the shame of economics, a logical structure of the greatest elegance which has only the most tenuous connections with the reality it is supposed to interpret.'

VERDICT

Businesses operate in a very dynamic competitive environment. Entrepreneurs in the theory of the firm are taken to act as if none of the objective conditions which confront them will change, for only on this assumption can they know what it would be like to be in equilibrium. But 'objective conditions' change constantly and this implies not content but discontent. Modern economics must abandon the concept of equilibrium as defined in the theory of the firm. Marginal costing has also become redundant in the Information Age with high-tech industries. Producing one computer chip costs millions of dollars but an additional chip costs very little. The firm's total cost becomes a fixed cost.

THE THEORY OF THE FIRM – A MODERN PERSPECTIVE

From managing maximum profit to managing complexity

In 1989 Rosabeth Moss Kanter, one of the well-known Harvard business gurus, published a book entitled *When Giants Learn To Dance*. In this book she writes about a revolution taking place in the business world, a revolution she calls 'post-entrepreneurial' because it applies entrepreneurial principles to the traditional corporation, creating a marriage between entrepreneurial creativity and corporate discipline. Kanter says that in the 1990s corporations must first make sure that all activities add value; they must find ways of getting more for less. Second, they must develop close working relationships with other organizations, extending the company's reach without increasing its size. Strategic alliances and partnerships are an effective way to do more with less. Third, post-entrepreneurial strategy is to promote new streams – a flow of new business possibilities within the firm. To do more with less means being able to capture and develop opportunities as they arise.

According to Kanter, the corporate olympics will be won by those who follow the four 'Fs' by being *Focused*, *Fast*, *Friendly* and *Flexible*.

In the 1990s many firms have tried to formulate their strategies and improve their operational effectiveness by being focused, fast, friendly and flexible. The present day economics of business organizations has to pay attention to the various ways organizations have adapted to maintain profitability and achieve corporate goals. Attention has to be focused on cost, outsourcing, competitive strategy, environmental scanning, quality, benchmarking, and the different dimensions of performance. The business world has become very complex. It is this complexity that is changing the paradigm in economics. The modern theory of the firm has to incorporate these initiatives and explore their economic perspectives.

> *The present day economics of business organizations has to pay attention to the various ways organizations have adapted to maintain profitability and achieve corporate goals.*

The cost curves in the traditional theory of the firm are based on the principles of diminishing returns and increasing returns to scale. The costs are neatly categorized into total, average and marginal costs. In practice, firms experiment with other cost strategies such as activity based costing.

Activity based costing

In the 1990s activity based costing (ABC) was adopted by many firms to focus their strategies on the cost drivers. Activity based costing builds up costs of activities first, then enables these costs to be directed to products/customers/regions on the basis of how these costs are driven. It should recognized that it is the activities and not the cost centres that create cost.

Activities are the tasks that people or machines perform in order to provide a product or service to a customer. An activity analysis enhances understanding of the complexities of a firm – it increases understanding of the work flow, it makes organizations aware of the role of each individual in the work flow and it brings about improvements in operating efficiency and customer service.

Costs are classified as activity costs, function sustaining costs, stepped costs and business sustaining costs. Activity costs are those costs which vary in direct proportion to volume. Function sustaining costs are those costs which are necessary to sustain a particular operation. Stepped costs are costs which do not change in direct proportion to volume changes but which can be analyzed by activity to specific volume levels. Business sustaining costs are costs which are necessary to continue in the business. The main focus is to examine the drivers of cost behind each group of activities. This system enables firms to cut out non-value added activities thus reducing inefficiencies, streamlining organizational structure, and identifying outsourcing options.

> *ABC provides an efficient way to organize the collection, processing and reporting of cost information that supports decision making and strategy formulation.*

ABC provides an efficient way to organize the collection, processing and reporting of cost information that supports decision making and strategy formulation. It yields accurate and relevant information for managers to improve the competitive position of their firms.

Not all firms have adopted ABC. However, increasingly as firms want to control costs, the focus of attention will be on activities and the cost drivers which are not highlighted in the traditional theory of the firm.

Outsourcing

Many organizations now use outsourcing as one of the key strategic options. According to David Bishop, Strategic Marketing Director of Ventura, outsourcing activity in the UK is worth between £2.5 billion and £3.2 billion and the market is forecast to grow a further 45 per cent by the year 2000.

Outsourcing has become recognized as an area of strategic importance.

Outsourcing involves using external organizations and specialists to undertake critical activities such as IT or customer service. Why do organizations outsource? Outsourcing delivers many advantages. It can:

- save costs
- reduce overheads
- provide access to specialist services
- gain a low cost entry to a new market
- improve operational efficiency
- free resources for critical services
- reduce pressure on resources internally
- provide access to economies of scale
- facilitate flat organizational structures
- improve quality.

Outsourcing has become recognized as an area of strategic importance. It is being seen less and less as a tactical, cost saving drive and more as a strategic direction that the organization follows. Organizations started outsourcing what were called peripheral services such as cleaning and catering. Nowadays they outsource critical areas of activities such as information systems, distribution, marketing, customer service and so on. According to some consultants, almost the entire value chain is open to the use of outside supply.

Competitive strategy

Firms in the modern business environment analyze the industrial and competitive environment within which they operate and make decisions as to what, how, when and for whom to produce.

According to Professor Michael Porter of Harvard University, competitive strategy involves positioning a business to maximize the value of the capabilities that distinguishes it from its competitors. Each firm is faced with five sets of forces governing its competitive positioning. These forces are:

- the industry
- entry and exit barriers
- substitutes
- the bargaining power of suppliers
- the bargaining power of buyers.

The interaction of these factors is reflected in the ultimate survival or success of the firm. Under each force there are significant factors which need to be analyzed in detail to conduct competitive analysis. For example, within the industry one needs to look at the number of players involved, the relative size of each player and their relative market share and power. Formulating successful strategy involves consideration of all these factors.

Michael Porter (1996) distinguishes between strategy and operational effectiveness:

> For almost two decades, managers have been learning to play by a new set of rules. Companies must be flexible to respond rapidly to competitive and market changes. They must benchmark continuously to achieve best practice. They must outsource aggressively to gain efficiencies. And they must nurture a few core competencies in the race to stay ahead of rivals.
>
> Positioning – once the heart of strategy – is rejected as too static for today's dynamic markets and changing technologies. According to the

new dogma, rivals can quickly copy any market position, and competitive advantage is, at best, temporary.

But those beliefs are dangerous half-truths, and they are leading more and more companies down the path of mutually destructive competition. True, some barriers to competition are falling as regulation eases and markets become global. True, companies have properly invested energy in becoming leaner and more nimble. In many industries, however, what some call hypercompetition is a self-inflicted wound, not the inevitable outcome of a changing paradigm of competition.

The root of the problem is the failure to distinguish between operational effectiveness and strategy. The quest for productivity, quality and speed has spawned a remarkable number of management tools and techniques: total management, benchmarking, timebased competition, outsourcing, partnering, reengineering, change management. Although the resulting operational improvements have often been dramatic, many companies have been frustrated by their inability to translate those gains into sustainable profitability. And bit by bit, almost imperceptibly, management tools have taken the place of strategy. As management push to improve on all fronts, they move farther away from viable competitive positions.

Operational effectiveness and strategy are both essential to superior performance, which, after all, is the primary goal of any enterprise.

Source: Reprinted by permission of *Harvard Business Review*. From Michael E. Porter, 'What is strategy?', *Harvard Business Review*, November–December, 1996, p. 61. Copyright 1996 by the President and Fellows of Harvard College; all rights reserved.

Adam M. Brandenburger of Harvard Business School and Barry J. Nalebuff (1995) of Yale School of Management advise companies to use game theory to shape their strategy:

The game of business is all about value: creating it and capturing it. Who are the participants in this enterprise? To describe them, we introduce the Value Net – a schematic map designed to represent all the players in the game and the interdependencies among them.

Interactions take place along two dimensions. Along the vertical dimension are the company's customers and suppliers. Resources such as labour and raw materials flow from the suppliers to the company, and products and services flow from the company to its customers. Money flows in the reverse direction from customers to the company and from the company to its suppliers. Along the horizontal dimension are the players with whom the company interacts but does not transact. They are its *substitutors* and *complementors.*

Substitutors are alternative players from whom customers may purchase products or to whom suppliers may sell their resources. Coca-Cola and PepsiCo are substitutors with respect to consumers because they sell rival colas. A little less obvious is that Coca-Cola and Tyson Foods are substitutors with respect to suppliers. This is because both companies use carbon dioxide. Tyson uses it for freezing chickens, and Coke uses it for carbonation. (As they say in the cola industry, 'No fizziness, no bizziness.')

Complementors are players from whom customers buy complementary products or to whom suppliers sell complementary resources. For example, hardware and software companies are classic complementors. Faster hardware, such as the Pentium chip, increases users' willingness to pay for more powerful software. More powerful software, such as the latest version of Microsoft Office, increases users' willingness to pay for faster hardware. American Airlines and United Airlines, though substitutors with respect to passengers, are complementors when they decide to update their fleets. That's because Boeing can recoup the cost of a new plane design only if enough airlines buy it. Since each airline effectively subsidises the other's purchase of planes, the two are complementors in this instance.

We introduce the term *substitutors* and *complementors* because we find that the traditional business vocabulary inhibits full understanding of the interdependencies that exist in business. If you call a player a competitor, you tend to focus on competing rather than on finding opportunities for co-operation. *Substitutors* describe the market relationship without that prejudice. Complementors, often overlooked in traditional strategic analysis, are the natural counterparts of substitutors.

The Value Net describes the various roles of the players. It's possible for the same player to occupy more than one role simultaneously.

Remember that American and United are both substitutors and complemetors. Gary Hamel and C.K. Prahalad make this point in *Competing for the Future* (Harvard Business School Press, 1994): 'On any given day . . . AT&T might find Motorola to be a supplier, a buyer, a competitor, and a partner.'

Source: Reprinted by permission of *Harvard Business Review*. From Adam Brandenburger and Barry J. Nalebuff, 'The right game: use game theory to shape strategy', *Harvard Business Review*, July–August, 1995, pp. 59–60. Copyright 1995 by the President and Fellows of Harvard College; all rights reserved.

The concept of complementarity is not new in economics. Various economists have presented them in discussing the concept of demand and consumers' equilibrium. They are discussed in relation to price and income effects. However, Brandenburger and Nalebuff present them within the context of business strategy.

Beware of competition!

On 6 May 1998, *USA Today* featured a story about Boeing which had made the mistake of disregarding the competition. Boeing first of all had upset some of its customers by not delivering planes as promised. Its engineers were not ready to meet the 1995 demand, and it was late in modernizing its production compared to its competitors. Production problems caused Boeing's first loss in 50 years in 1997 – first quarter profits plunged 91 per cent from 1997's first quarter. Boeing has to take serious note of competition and improve its operational efficiency if it is to compete effectively.

Environmental scanning

An organization's effectiveness depends on how it adapts to macro environmental factors. These are sociological factors, technological factors, environmental factors and political factors (STEP factors).

Sociological factors relate to changes taking place in a society – changes in values, tastes, attitudes, life styles and so on. Technological factors incorporate changes made possible by computers, telecommunications, the Internet, e-mail and so on. Economic factors reflect the changing economic landscape and include purchasing power, employment, inflation, savings, investment, the introduction of the Euro etc. Political factors involve changes in political ideologies, privatization and the deregulation policies of various governments.

STEP factors in general have had a significant impact on the way businesses are conducted these days. For example, changing political ideologies and a climate of co-operation have facilitated various joint ventures and 'borderless organizations'. The business world is full of globalization stories involving global sourcing and global manufacturing which are impacting business strategies of many organizations.

Firms should scan the total environment including all the STEP factors in order to adapt their strategies. Strategic adaptation has to be the key goal of any organization that has to sustain profitability and retain competitive advantage.

Total quality management

Total quality management became one of the most pervasive aspects of business management in the 1980s. Firms focused their attention on continuous improvement in order to meet service excellence. Quality gurus like Joseph M. Juran and W. Edwards Deming believed that in order to be competitive, quality must be the foundation of everything businesses do. As far back as 1951 Japan created the Deming Prize which was concerned with total quality. It was not until 1987 that the US instituted the Baldridge Award urging organizations to improve their quality practices and performance. Organizations which have entered for the award have to satisfy examiners in the following areas: leadership, information and analysis, strategic quality planning, human resources utilization, quality assurance of product and services, quality results and customer satisfaction.

For many organizations it was important to win the Baldridge Award in order to gain more customers. In Europe the European

Quality Award was introduced in 1988 as a result of an initiative by fourteen European businesses. European businesses have to satisfy the European Foundation for Quality Management in the areas of leadership, people management, policy and strategy, resources, processes, people satisfaction, customer satisfaction, impact on society and business results. The first European Quality Award was won by Rank Xerox in 1992.

Many organizations started total quality initiatives a number of years ago. It is not a quick-fix solution to improving operational or product or service efficiency. Rank Xerox launched a worldwide programme in 1989 called 'Leadership through Quality'. ICL started its quality initiatives in 1986 whereas for Miliken, the quality initiative began in 1981. Quality to these companies is not a destination but a journey.

> *Quality to these companies is not a destination but a journey.*

These initiatives delivered significant improvements for these companies. The success stories acted as incentives for suppliers to embark upon the total quality journey. Miliken, for example, suggested to Ciba Geigy, the Swiss chemical giant, that the company should adopt total quality management practices. Toyota asked Philips Electronics to improve its quality in supplying headlamps. Philips, which made light bulbs for Honda, was told that its defect rate of one faulty bulb in fifty was not good enough. Philips met and even exceeded Honda's requirements.

A distinction should be made between the efficiency and effectiveness of a firm or organization. Efficiency is doing the right thing whereas effectiveness is doing the right thing right. Fig. 5.9 highlights the distinction. An organization which monitors and achieves its corporate goals very efficiently is an effective organization. Effectiveness should be the target aimed at by all organizations in order to achieve business success.

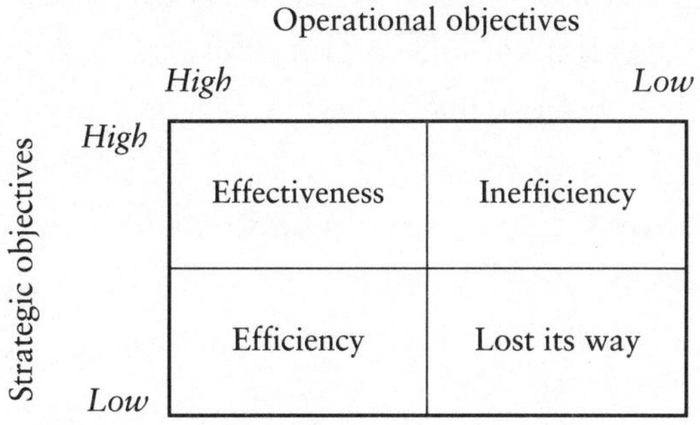

Operational objectives

	High	Low
High	Effectiveness	Inefficiency
Low	Efficiency	Lost its way

Strategic objectives (High / Low, vertical axis label)

Fig. 5.9 Operational objectives

In addition, there are other quality management systems such as ISO 9000 that firms adopt in order to improve their quality standards and win customers.

Benchmarking

Benchmarking is a method of improving business performance by learning from other organizations how to do things better in order to be the 'best in class'. Rank Xerox defines benchmarking as 'a continuous systematic process of evaluating companies recognized as industry leaders, to determine business and work processes that represent "best practice" and establish performance goals.'

Some organizations undertake benchmarking in order to ensure that their businesses' process goals are set to achieve the best qualitative results achieved by world class leaders and to incorporate best practice throughout their organizations.

Benchmarking originated in the US approximately two decades ago. Now 95 per cent of US companies say they are practising benchmarking. In the late 1970s, Xerox, who are recognized as being the originator of benchmarking, found that the retail price of Canon photocopiers was lower than Xerox's manufacturing costs. They sent a benchmarking team to Japan to compare their performance in a wide range of areas with their Japanese counterparts and returned to undertake the 'step change' needed to catch up. Benchmarking thus began in Xerox in 1979 and it became a company-wide effort in 1981.

As far as Europe is concerned, benchmarking seems to be well established. Coopers & Lybrand undertook a survey in 1994 covering the Times 1000 companies or their equivalent across five European countries – namely, the UK, the Netherlands, Switzerland, Spain and France. The survey showed that over two-thirds of companies in the UK, the Netherlands and Switzerland, over half of French companies and a third of Spanish companies are using benchmarking techniques to improve their performance.

Dimensions of business performance

Business performance is affected by a variety of factors. How well a company performs depends on STEP factors, competition and customers. These are all external factors. Internally, the performance of an organization depends on leadership, employees, customers and corporate values.

Effective leadership

Effective leadership nowadays involves shifting from a power-driven attitude to a responsibility-driven attitude involving the ability to build effective teams, to provide effective communication, to be able to listen to employees and customers and to promote organizational and people development. Employees now look for leaders who are credible and who have integrity – leaders they can trust.

> *Internally, the performance of an organization depends on leadership, employees, customers and corporate values.*

Employees

Employees are one of the major stakeholders for every organization. Unlike technology and capital, this resource (people) has expectations and aspirations and they are manifested in behaviour which has a significant impact on business performance. Employees should feel, 'I'm OK, you're OK' in order to deliver corporate and departmental or divisional objectives (*see* Fig. 5.10).

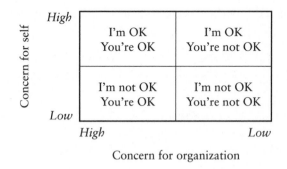

Fig. 5.10

Organizations have to pay special attention to measuring the performance of their employees and to invest in their development. It is said that 'people mean profit'.

Customers

Winning performance is a matter of meeting customers' needs. Delivering 'service excellence' has become the business cliché of the 1990s. Businesses have to learn to get 'close to the customers' to make sure of their survival. Companies like ABB, Canon Europe, Motorola, Rank Xerox, ICL and Avis make sure they have mechanisms in place to receive customer feedback and to act on it. Organizations that adopt customer-focused strategy have to undergo a fundamental change in their beliefs and values. Everyone in the organization has to undergo and live by new beliefs and values.

Organizations make attempts to get close to customers by:

- creating a customer focus group which involves forming panels of customers to give feedback on products, service and competitors
- visiting customers
- sending out questionnaires and undertaking postal or telephone surveys
- commissioning customer research.

At this stage it is important to note that a satisfied customer is not enough. Satisfied customers often do not come back. Xerox discovered that if satisfaction is ranked on a one-to-five scale from completely dissatisfied to completely satisfied, those with a rank of four – though satisfied – are six times more likely to defect than those with a rank of five.

Thomas A. Stewart (1997) says:

We are used to thinking – assuming really – that satisfaction and loyalty move in tandem, like handholding young lovers. The assumption's wrong. Satisfaction and loyalty are more like such famously wary pairs as Lizzie and Darcy of *Pride and Prejudice*, Beatrice and Benedick in *Much Ado About Nothing*, or even Cramden and Norton. In vigorously competitive markets, a graph – with satisfaction on the horizontal axis and retention on the vertical axis – doesn't rise diagonally. Instead it dawdles along a curve. Loyalty rises a bit as satisfaction increases, swooping abruptly up only at the highest levels of satisfaction. In monopolistic or oligopolistic markets the curve goes the other way; since these customers are more or less stuck, loyalty – if that's the word – rises steeply even at low levels of satisfaction, inching up only a little more at the highest levels.

Which gives you two strategies: neuter competition or satisfy customers completely. One way to create uncompetitive markets is to limit customers' choice. Patents do that, as do regulation, airport landing rights, broadcast licenses, mergers that tiptoe past the sleeping dogs of Justice, and the like. You can also maim the Invisible Hand by making it inconvenient or expensive for customers to switch. Frequent-flier plans are a great example, so powerful that few airlines even try to make flying pleasant. Location is another: I prefer Burger King to McDonald's but when my cholesterol is too low I go to McDonalds because it is closer. De facto standards also raise switching costs. The ubiquity of Windows, the dollar, and gasoline-powered-cars makes it harder to switch to Macs, the lira, or electric vehicles.

Thomas A. Stewart also writes:

> It is wiser not to follow customer feedback lavishly. Companies like Chrysler, Compaq, and Motorola have achieved startling successes by ignoring their customers from time to time. Chrysler for instance forged ahead with the original minivan despite research showing that people recoiled at such an odd-looking vehicle. Compaq bet millions on PC network servers in the early 1990s even though customers said they would never abandon their mainframes.
>
> Source: *Fortune*. Copyright 1997. Time Inc. All rights reserved.

Customer satisfaction accompanied by customer loyalty has become the cornerstone of retaining customers and strengthening any organization's customer base.

Corporate values

Corporate vision and corporate values drive business performance. In 1992 a survey of business executives' opinion in the UK on 'Corporate Values – the Bottom Line Contribution' was undertaken by John Humble in association of Digital Equipment Co. The survey stated: 'Corporate values are the key to management of change. They are the "glue" which binds together today's flattened, decentralized, international structures. Corporate leaders need to develop and implement values that are appropriate to the vision of strategies of the company, and ultimately to those of the company's stakeholders, including customers, employees and shareholders.'

Qualitative and quantitative performance goals

The traditional theory of the firm focused its attention on one objective, i.e. profit maximization. The focus of attention gradually shifted to concentrating on profitability rather than maximization of profit. The accounting system involved measuring and analyzing key financial indicators such as return on capital employed, profit margin, asset turnover, stock turnover, cash flow, debtor and creditor days, and current ratios in order to track down financial performance. Until the late 1990s the emphasis has been on financial performance.

However, creating shareholder value is gradually becoming a mantra for many top managements today because they believe that the ultimate aim of a business is to generate value for its shareholders in the form of financial returns. Two financial measures are gaining in popularity: economic value added (EVA) and market value added (MVA).

Today's cry is to enhance shareholder value.

EVA is presented as a new theory of corporate performance. It measures how management has increased or decreased the value of capital. EVA is after-tax net operating profit minus cost of capital. A positive EVA signifies an increase in the value of capital for shareholders. MVA is a measure of wealth a company has created for investors. It is the difference between total market value and invested capital. EVA/MVA measurements are undertaken by companies like Coca-Cola, AT&T, Eli Lilly, Lucas-Varity and so on.

In the past, companies have always managed and measured performance on behalf of their owners (stockholders). When the 'managerial revolution' came about, divorcing ownership from control, managers were appointed to run businesses on behalf of their owners, the shareholders. Today's cry is to enhance shareholder value.

However, some writers now think that there are other stakeholders whose interests must be considered. These are employees, customers, suppliers and in some instances the community and government. Some argue that it is a duty of the directors to give due weight to all stakeholders. This would mean that organizations have to come up with performance measures accommodating interests of all key stakeholders.

Performance measurement using the Balancd Scorecard approach

In 1992 Professor Robert Kaplan of Harvard Business School and Dr David P. Norton of Renaissance Strategy Group put forward a new approach to measuring an organization's performance. This was the Balanced Scorecard. Measurement is undertaken from the following key perspectives:

- Financial perspective: How should we appear to our shareholders?
- Customers' perspective: How should we appear to our customers?
- Internal processes perspective: What businesses processes must we excel at?
- Growth and learning perspective: How will we sustain our ability to change?

The above four perspectives focus attention on internal as well as external drivers to performance.

The Balanced Scorecard approach with some variations is used by companies such as AT&T, Co-operative Bank, W. H. Smith, S. G. Warburg, Eurotunnel and so on. The centre piece of the Balanced Scorecard is the corporate mission and strategy. The scorecard translates mission and corporate strategy throughout the organization. It enables organizations to track financial measures while simultaneously monitoring progress in intangible areas of business which have become important in today's business climate.

Managing complexity in a real world

In *Business Week* (May 1998) there was a story about Unilever's new strategy as far as emerging markets were concerned. It was reported that the company was investing heavily to develop key products such as ice cream, tea, margarine, skin care, personal-wash products and some prestige products such as Calvin Klein fragrances. Its aim is to push for growth in Central and Eastern Europe, China, South East Asia, Latin America and India.

Companies often have to formulate strategies in the face of diverse challenges in order to remain competitive in a global market. *Business Week* (February 1998) also reported a story of AT&T's new strategy. AT&T's new chief executive officer, Armstrong, was moving fast to cut costs and reposition AT&T for the digital age. His main target was to reduce AT&T's overhead costs from 29 per cent of revenue to the industry average which is 22 per cent of revenue. Armstrong was determined to make the company's wireless operation more profitable and enhance its international operations.

Managing complexity – the story of Nokia

Leif Sjöblom (1999) looks at how four forces – change in consumer expectations, technological change, deregulation and regional forces – impact the telecommunications industry:

> The primary sources of change in telecoms have been deregulation and technological change. Some 21 years ago, telecoms was considered a 'natural monopoly' where the investment in infrastructure was so huge that it was not desirable to allow competition and duplication. This resulted in protected national operators for post, telegraph and telephones – PTTs – that had a high cost structure and poor customer service.
>
> The breakthrough in digital technology has dramatically reduced the infrastructure costs and made open competition economically feasible. At the same time, consumer demands have changed from the standard 'fixed line voice entry' to mobile telephony, the Internet and a proliferation of other services.
>
> And again, although segments such as mobile communication grow rapidly world-wide, most of the growth has happened in Asia.
>
> The changes have created two types of operator: the former PTTs,

with a high cost structure and poor marketing skills; and new greenfield operators with a lower cost structure and, often, excellent marketing skills.

Yet although the PTTs have struggled in the changing environment, they have fared reasonably well in the competition. However, the clear winner is the consumer.

In the first six years after the UK market was opened up, for example, the service level increased dramatically while prices decreased in real terms by about 6 per cent annually.

Although the operator business is still primarily local, the telecom equipment supplier business has long been global.

Fast growing companies are the ones that have focused on new services, such as mobile telephony. Completely new players such as Nokia, which was not even on the top 10 list a few years ago, are now among the fastest growing and profitable companies in the industry.

Nokia has enjoyed its phenomenal success by exploiting the forces for change in the industry. Ten years ago it was a small, diversified conglomerate with a very small domestic market. It predicted the growth in telecoms and transformed itself into a pure telecom company.

Because of its small domestic market, the growth had to be international. That implied the development of a completely new set of competencies – particularly the ability to compete in the most competitive global markets.

Nokia has always had an excellent technological reputation. However, a major part of its success is its understanding of market changes.

In the new deregulated industry, Nokia knew that a different type of consumer – the 'greenfield operator' – would emerge. This type of customer's needs and expectations would be very different from those of an established PTT.

The new operator would create value by managing the customer interface, by providing excellent customer service and by continually innovating and introducing new services. They would focus on marketing (their core competency) and expect suppliers to provide complete technical solutions that could differentiate them from the PTTs. The key to serving this segment was an ability to convert the latest technology into products and services that would be adopted by the end-user. By making an early entry into the most competitive markets – Asia and the newly deregulated UK – and by focusing on the new operators, Nokia has gained an excellent understanding of changing end-user needs. That understanding can now be leveraged into new products and services based on the latest technology.

Changing consumers' expectations, technological developments, deregulation and regional forces have become important sources of competition. Organizations have to learn to manage them in order to survive in an intensely competitive climate.

VERDICT

Apart from focusing its attention on profit maximization and attaining equilibrium, firms in practice have to deal with numerous strategies in order to manage their businesses in a world which is becoming increasingly complex. Such complexity necessitates new paradigms and new thinking on firms' strategy. Equilibrium positions become temporary phenomena in a fast-changing complex world. Firms constantly need to adapt to a changing external environment.

THE NEW APPROACH TO ECONOMICS

In a most thought-provoking article Eric D. Beinhocker (1997) writes:

Modern neo-classical microeconomics was founded in the 1870s by Leon Walras, William Stanley Jevons, and Carl Menger, and synthesised into a coherent theory by Alfred Marshall at the turn of the century. Seeking to make economics more scientific, Walras, Jevons and Menger had borrowed ideas and mathematical apparatus from the leading science of their day, energy physics. Twenty years earlier Julius Mayer, James

Prescott Joule, Hermann von Helmholtz, and Ludwig August had achieved breakthroughs in energy physics that paved the way for thermodynamics. The early neo-classicist copied the mathematics of mid-nineteenth-century energy physics equation by equation, translating it metaphorically (and, according to many physicists incorrectly) into economic concepts.

Another neoclassicist, Irving Fisher, showed in his 1892 doctoral thesis how the physicists' 'particle' became the economists' 'individual', 'force' became 'marginal utility', 'kinetic energy' became 'total expenditure', and so on. Although microeconomic theory has undergone many changes over the past century, the core ideas developed by Alfred Marshall, Irving Fisher, and the other early neo-classicists still resonate in economics textbooks today.

Here can be found the roots of management's family tree, from Mayer and early thermodynamics through Marshall and microeconomics to Michael Porter and the five forces model of strategy. This intellectual lineage still affects the way we approach management today.

Equilibrium systems

The Argentinean writer Jorge Luis Borges observed, 'It may be that universal history is the history of a handful of metaphors.' The mid-nineteenth-century energy physicists developed what may be one of the great metaphors of all time: that of closed equilibrium systems. Closed equilibrium systems are the core metaphor of Alfred Marshall's traditional economics and much of our management thinking today.

Consider a ball at the bottom of a bowl. If no energy or mass enters or leaves the bowl – that is, the system is closed – the ball will sit in equilibrium at the bottom of the bowl for ever. In economic terms, the sides of our bowl represent the structure of a market (for instance, producer costs and consumer preferences), and the gravity that pulls the ball to its lowest energy state represents profit-seeking behaviour pulling firms to their highest profit state. If we know the economic forces at work, and if firms are rational, we can predict where the ball will come to rest in the bowl – in other words, the prices, quantities produced, and profitability of firms under equilibrium. If some exogenous shock now hits the system (say a technology shift alters producer costs), the sides of the bowl change shape, and the ball rolls to a new point of equilibrium.

This sequence of equilibrium – change a variable – new equilibrium is what economists call comparative statics, and forms the underpinning of Alfred Marshall's economics and most business strategy. In a typical strategy analysis, a company will look at its position in the current industry structure, consider the shocks and changes that are occurring or might occur, and then develop a point of view on how the industry is likely to change and what that will mean for its own strategy.

Such an approach makes three important assumptions: that the industry structure is known, that diminishing returns apply, and that all firms are perfectly rational. But what happens if rapid technological or business-system innovation makes producer costs and consumer preferences uncertain? What if we face not diminishing returns (where each additional acre of soybean planted is on poorer land and thus yields a lower return), but increasing returns (where each extra Netscape browser sold increases the value of the World Wide Web and thus yields a higher return)?* What if firms lack complete information, or different firms interpret the same information in different ways?

If the fundamental assumptions underlying the equilibrium model are relaxed the effect on the ball in the bowl will be dramatic. The sides of the bowl start to bend and flex, losing their smooth shape and becoming a landscape of hills and valleys, and the ball can no longer tell which way is up. Now it is impossible to predict where the ball will roll, and Alfred Marshall loses his equilibrium. But this is not merely a theoretical problem, since the ball-in-the-bowl equilibrium model is the basis for our strategy ideas.

Marshall's equilibrium model was a reasonable approximation to the agricultural and manufacturing economy of his time, and it is still useful in many situations. But it runs into trouble in today's dynamic high-tech

---

* For a more detailed discussion of increasing returns, see W. Brian Arthur, 'Positive feedbacks in the economy.' *The McKinsey Quarterly*, 1994, Number 1, pp. 81–95, and 'Increasing returns and the new world of business,' *Harvard Business Review*, July–August 1996, pp. 100–9.

and service-dominated economy. Consider a company that plans to invade heavily in entering a new market. It faces strong incumbents that enjoy a host of competitive advantages such as scale and brands, and that already compete fiercely with each other. Moreover, its own value proposition, while distinct from competitors', can easily be copied. In short, the entrant has no obvious source of sustainable competitive advantage. Any observer taking a traditional view of strategy would surely question the sanity of making this investment.

But what if the entrant were CNN? Dell Computer? Wal-Mart? or IKEA? All these companies succeeded in spite of what the traditional model of strategy would perceive as long odds. They all violated the closed-equilibrium assumptions at the heart of this model. They innovated in products and/or business systems, took advantage of increasing returns dynamics, and had mental models of their industry that were radically different from those of incumbent competitors.

One might use traditional strategy frameworks to explain the success of these companies retrospectively, but it is often much harder to use them to look forward in industries undergoing rapid change. A Porter or SCP analysis will be of only limited help to, say, a telecom CEO facing deregulation, profound technological change, industry convergence, globalization, and increasing returns in sectors like the Internet and wireless. What this CEO needs is a model of a world where innovation, change and uncertainty, rather than equilibrium, are the natural state of things.

Complex adaptive systems

Anthills are marvellous things. With elaborate labyrinths of tunnels, layouts reflecting their occupants' social hierarchies, chambers dedicated to specific functions, and carefully cited entrances and exits, they are as thoughtfully constructed as any condominium complex. Yet who is the engineer? Where is the blueprint?

The answer, of course, is that there isn't one. The plan for the anthill does not exist in any individual ant. Rather, each ant is programmed by its DNA to obey a set of relatively simple rules, such as 'stand between two other ants and pass along anything that is handed to you.' Ants communicate with each other via chemical signals known as pheromones. These signals provide inputs and outputs for the rules, and switch them on and off. It is the dynamic interaction of the rules and signals that creates the anthill structure.

The community of ants is an example of a *complex adaptive system*. Such systems share three characteristics:

First, they are *open, dynamic systems*. The Marshall ball-in-a-bowl system is closed; no energy or mass enters or leaves, and the system is able to settle into an equilibrium state. By contrast, a complex adaptive system is always open, and the energy and mass that constantly flow through it keep it in dynamic disequilibrium. An anthill is a perpetual-motion machine in which patterns of behaviour are constantly shifting; some patterns appear stable, others chaotic.

Second, they are made up of *interacting agents*. These agents might be ants, people, molecules or computer programs. Systems that have one agent – say, a monopoly model in economics, or a body in motion in physics – tend to be fairly simple and predictable. Similarly systems that have multitudes of agents that are all the same – as with perfect competition in economics, or gases in physics – are also simple and predictable. But systems that have somewhere between one and a multitude of agents, or systems where the agents are all different, such as real-world business markets, are complex and difficult to predict.

This complexity derives from the dynamic interactions of the agents: what each agent does affects one or more others, at least some of the time. The interactions of agents in a complex system are guided by rules: laws of physics, codes of conduct, or economic imperatives such as 'cut the price if your competitor does.' If the repertoire of rules is fixed, the result is a *complex system*. If the rules are evolving, as with genes encoded in DNA or the strategies pursued by players in a game, the result is a *complex adaptive system*.

Third, complex adaptive systems exhibit *emergence and self-organisation*. As individuals, ants don't do much. But put them in a group where they can interact and an anthill emerges. Because the anthill rises out of the bottom-up dynamic interactions of the ants and not from a top-down

master plan, it is said to self-organise. The emergent structure is independent of specific agents. Individual ants may come and go, but the
pattern of the anthill persists.

The new economics

. . . A number of economists are beginning to say that economies are complex adaptive systems, rather than the closed equilibrium systems they
have long been thought to be. The case has yet to be proven, but there is
both circumstantial evidence and support from some eminent economists,
among them Kenneth Arrow, a Nobel Prize winner and one of the prime
architects of the modern neo-classical model, and Brian Arthur of the
Santa Fe Institute. Indeed the new economics is sometimes referred to as
the Santa Fe school of economics after the interdisciplinary research
center to which many economists working on ideas of complexity are
affiliated.

Past attempts by academics and popular business gurus to take an evo-
lutionary or biological view of economic systems have mostly been
metaphorical, and have failed. By contrast, the complexity economists are
saying not just that economies are like biological systems, but that the two
spheres follow the same deep laws. To be sure, these laws will not play
out in quite the same way in economics and in biology, but if we can
improve our understanding of them, we will gain valuable insights into
the working of markets and firms.

Source: Reprinted with permission of the publisher from Eric D. Beinhocker, 'Strategy at the edge of
chaos', *The McKinsey Quarterly*, 1997, No. 1, pp. 26–30. Copyright 1997 McKinsey & Company. All
rights reserved.

The article goes on to say that the key components of new economics will be *wisdom* underpinning cognitive behaviour, *webs* of
dynamic relationships and *waves* embodying ripple effects (multi-
plier effect). The language used ('wisdom', 'webs', 'waves') to describe
the behaviour of the firm reflects the change that has taken place in
dealing with 'the theory of the firm'.

```
┌──────────────┤ VERDICT ├──────────────┐
│                                                              │
│  Marshall's equilibrium model has no place in the economics of │
│  the information age. The business world is moving so fast that to │
│  talk of equilibrium is to ignore the innovative and the fast- │
│  moving world in which we live.                              │
│                                                              │
└──────────────────────────────────────────┘
```

EXECUTIVE SUMMARY

- The theory of the firm in traditional economics is based on the assumptions that entrepreneurs want to maximize profits. To maximize profit a firm's marginal cost and its marginal revenue must be equal. This is the firm's equilibrium position.

- The theory is surrounded by various other assumptions which do not bear resemblance to the real world.

- Putting a modern perspective to the theory of the firm involves examining various initiatives undertaken by organizations in order to compete effectively. These initiatives include focusing on strategy, paying attention to changing sociological, technological, economic and political factors, focusing on different types of costs, outsourcing, adopting benchmarking practice, total quality management and measuring organizational performance effectively. Organizations' performance depends on effective leadership, employees, customers and corporate values.

- The various initiatives are geared to make firms focused, flexible and fast.

- Many companies today face dilemmas and challenges and they have to come up with appropriate strategies to respond to the challenges, for example how Nokia managed a complex situation to succeed.

- Complexity in the business environment has prompted some writers to come up with a new approach to economics – *adopting a complex adaptive system.*

References

Beinhocker, Eric D. (1997) 'Strategy at the edge of chaos', *McKinsey Quarterly*, 1, 26–30.

Brandenburger, Adam M. and Nalebuff, Barry J. (1995) 'The right game: use game theory to shape strategy', *Harvard Business Review*, July–August, 59–60.

Downie, Jack (1958) *The Competitive Process*. London: Duckworth.

Elstorm, P. (1998) 'New Boss New Plan', *Business Week*, 2 February, 118–21.

Porter, Michael (1996) 'What is strategy?', *Harvard Business Review*, November–December, 61.

Reed, Stanley (1998) 'Unilever Finally Knows Where It's Going East', *Business Week*, 4 May, 18–21.

Sjöblom, Leif (1999) 'Success lies one step ahead of the consumer' in *FT Mastering Gobal Business*. London: Financial Times Management, 39–42.

Stewart, Thomas (1997) 'A Satisfied Customer Isn't Enough', *Fortune*, 21 July, 69–71.

NEW PERSPECTIVES ON THE FACTORS OF PRODUCTION I

Competence and customers

What the customer thinks he is buying, what he considers 'value' is decisive – it determines what a business is, what it produces, and whether it will prosper.

Peter Drucker

Human assets shouldn't be misused. Brains are becoming the core of organisations – other activities can be contracted out.

Charles Handy

INTRODUCTION

L and, labour and capital have traditionally constituted the factors of production in economics. Over the years the composition of land, labour and capital has changed. They no longer play an important part in creating the wealth of a nation. What matters now is the competencies that exist within organizations, the customers and the intelligent workforce, who combine to create the wealth of a nation. 'Intangibles' are taking over from 'tangibles' and we are increasingly forced to adopt a different mindset when considering the true factors of production in a modern but changing business environment.

Various cases cited in this book have shown the importance of competencies and customers. The time has now come to discard land, labour and capital as factors of production and in their place consider competencies, customers and knowledge as instrumental factors of production.

WHO CREATES VALUE IN ECONOMIC PRODUCTION?

In economics the purpose of production is to create utilities by providing goods and services to meet consumer demand. The resources that are used as inputs are known as factors of production. These resources are categorized into land, labour, capital and enterprise.

As their rewards, land earns rent, labour earns wages, capital earns interest and enterprise, as a reward for taking risks, gets profit. Economic theory is more concerned with what determines the prices of the factors of production than with what determines their respective shares of the national income. The analysis of the pricing of factors of production is parallel to the analysis of the pricing of commodities and services incorporating marginal analysis. Again the analysis is undertaken within the context of key assumptions. It is assumed that throughout the analysis technical conditions are given and constant and that the factors of production are used and combined as efficiently as possible. Beyond a certain point of their utilization all these factors of production yield diminishing returns.

However, the world has moved on since the categorization of factors of production into land, labour, capital and enterprise. The economy is changing; jobs are changing; the workforce is changing. Professor Danny Quah of the London School of Economics has put forward the notion of a 'weightless economy' where people are willing to pay for activities, products and services which are intangible. Economic value created in a weightless economy is 'infinitely expandable' and has the property of being 'inappropriable'. We have moved from the 'agricultural age' through the 'industrial age' to the 'information age'. The whole nature of the economy, and in particular microeconomics, is being transformed. At macro level the nature of work is changing.

In May 1998, the British Government urged employers to be more family-friendly. The Green Paper on childcare will draw attention to the importance of developing ways to make work more user-friendly, in particular making it easier to balance the demands of a healthy social and family life with productive and efficient working practices.

The attitude of young employees are also changing. A survey conducted by Coopers and Lybrand has shown that young people value their personal life as much as their professional life. Price Waterhouse enable their staff to organize themselves to do the job in whatever way they think fit.

Neil Harris, Programme Manager for Flexible Working, Digital Equipment Co. UK, presented the following information on Digital's flexible working practices at *The Economist* Conferences on 19

November 1993. According to him, Digital Equipment developed a strategy to use flexible working as a way to improve its business performance. This strategy focused on the key performance indicators of productivity and asset utilization through the establishment of what are called 'high performance (flexible) work teams'. The teams' objectives were well-defined and infrastructure services were put in place to promote 'open' working environments to support 'virtual' team working.

What Digital called 'Location Independent Working' was introduced to integrate the rationalization of office space with the working of 'virtual' teams. Location Independent Working is based on the principle that services are provided from a centre by support staff, themselves high performance teams, on an 'as needed' basis.

The technology developed by Digital to allow Location Independent Working was based on the integration of computers and telephony, called CIT. There was also a voice processor and fax interface. At the heart of the system was a leading-edge software integration capability that enabled e-mail, voice mail and fax mail to be accessed through a common interface, either a PC/terminal or a phone. This meant that users could access their voice mail via the computer or their e-mail via the phone.

Similar strategies have been adopted by many organizations since the mid 1990s. In 1994, some 32 000 employees of AT&T stayed at home 'telecommuting'.

Tangible and intangible economics

Mahlon Apgar (1998) explores the pros and cons of the alternative workplace (AW). He writes about tangible and intangible economics:

Managers should look at the economics of potential AW programmes from three perspectives – the company's, the employee's and the customer's – and weigh the tangible and intangible costs against the respective benefits. Tangible set up costs for the company include hardware, software, training, and any equipment or furniture, the company provides; ongoing costs include allowances, phone charges, and technical support. In home offices, employees provide their own space and some, if not all, of the furnishing and equipment. Intangible costs for the company and its employees include the time spent learning new work habits and ways of communicating with colleagues and customers.

Aside from real estate savings, the organization benefits from increased employee productivity, recruiting, and retention – usually because AW employees have both more professional and more personal time. In one AT&T unit, for example, the average AW participant gained almost five weeks per year by eliminating a 50-minute daily commute. Employees in home offices and other remote locations also can be more efficient during the workday because they have fewer distractions and less down time . . . Customer satisfaction also improves as customers become comfortable communicating with the organization electronically; they can reach employees more quickly and receive more direct, personal attention.

Employee satisfaction is linked with customer satisfaction and improved performance.

Intangible benefits include closer teamwork and greater flexibility. The simple act of removing the walls that separate people in traditional private offices often fosters teamwork . . . A crucial intangible benefit of an AW programme is the value that employees place on increased personal time and control. Although they tend to work longer hours and may even have difficulty leaving their home offices, AW employees find the promise of flexibility attractive, so they are easier to recruit and retain . . . Indeed any organization adopting an AW initiative can be expected to reach a new plateau – with lower fixed costs, higher productivity, and greater employee and customer satisfaction than it previously experienced.

Source: Reprinted by permission of *Harvard Business Review*. From Mahlon Apgar, IV. 'The alternative workplace: changing where and how people work', *Harvard Business Review*, May–June, 1998, p. 128. Copyright 1998 by the President and Fellows of Harvard College; all rights reserved.

Apgar emphasizes the need to look at the workplace from the point of view of the company (competencies), employees (knowledge) and customers. Intangible factors now matter as much as, if not more than, tangible factors. More attention has to be paid to employees and their satisfaction in order to deliver service excellence. Employee satisfaction is linked with customer satisfaction and improved performance.

Six trends that will reshape the workplace

According to *Fortune*, May 1993, the following six trends will reshape the workplace as we move towards the new millennium:

- the average company will become smaller, employing fewer people;
- the traditional hierarchical organization will give way to a variety of organizational forms, the network of specialists foremost among these;
- technicians, ranging from computer repairers to radiation therapists, will replace manufacturing operatives as the worker élite;
- the vertical division of labour will be replaced by a horizontal division;
- the paradigm of doing business will shift from making a product to providing a service;
- work itself will be redefined: constant learning, more high-order thinking, less nine-to-five.

Charles Handy (1995) has put forward the view that a lot of employees in the future will become 'portfolio workers', selling their skills to a variety of clients and all of us will be looking beyond work to find meaning and identity. According to Handy, the twentieth century will be known as 'the century of organization'. He put forward the notion of 'half-by-two-by-three' – that is, future

> *Future organizations will have half the workers, paid twice as well, producing three times as much.*

organizations will have half the workers, paid twice as well, producing three times as much. The other half will be outside the organization and those with competent skills will become independent workers selling back into the organization for the most part, but also into several other organizations at the same time.

People power

Labour as a factor of production has been transformed significantly since the days of neo-classical economists. Most employees are now empowered. Empowerment became one of the key business buzz words in the early 1990s. Companies like Motorola, AT&T, ICL, BP and Miliken have all improved their business performance by empowering their employees.

Professor Rosabeth Moss Kanter (1983) emphasized the need for people in organizations to work as 'corporate entrepreneurs'. The top management should learn to trust their people to make decisions and take responsibility. Empowerment is about creating situations where workers share power and assume the responsibility of making decisions for the benefit of organizations and themselves.

Organizations have realized that they need to 'empower' their employees in order to deliver service excellence.

In the business world today, organizations have to pay special attention to customers. Those who have remained in the delayered and downsized organizations have to respond very swiftly to customers' demands and needs. Organizations have realized that they need to 'empower' their employees in order to deliver service excellence.

In a survey on empowerment, conducted by Harbridge Consulting Group Ltd in 1994, it was found that empowerment in organizations brings about the following benefits:

- increased motivation, commitment, energy and enthusiasm
- improved customer focus

- job enrichment, increased sense of ownership
- reduced staff turnover
- improved financial contribution
- increased innovation
- greater flexibility
- higher skill levels
- improved individual performance
- lower administrative costs
- better ability to cope with change.

However, those employees at the top of organizations are experiencing different kinds of changes as far as financial rewards are concerned. Executive (top) pay is growing much faster than pay to other employees and the economy as a whole, according to Ken Hugessen of William Mercer. Talking at *The Economist* Conferences in February 1998, he said:

> To understand why, we need to consider the underlying market dynamics – a new paradigm in executive compensation.
>
> The new paradigm is in place in the US; proven talent is being 'priced' by reference to the capital markets; under this paradigm, investors and Boards of Directors are determining pay for executives on their expected contribution to increasing shareholder value. No longer is pay solely by reference to what other executives earn. Rather, it is set anticipating the amount of wealth the executives can create for shareholders, and the high pay is essential to keep these already wealthy executives interested in working!

He gave examples of annual CEO compensation during 1996. Dunlap of Sunbeam received $11.3 million, Gerstner of IBM $20.9 million, Bossidy of Allied Signal $22.8 million, Welch of General Electric $24.4 million and Eisner of Disney $55.1 million. However, in the cases of Disney, General Electric, IBM and Allied Signals company value increased by billions of dollars.

Global Finance (September 1996) gave information on the best paid UK finance directors. Hans Eggerstedt, a finance director, was reported to have been paid in total £636,000 in 1995. Hugh Collum of SmithKline Beecham was reported to have received a total remuneration of £600,000. Nigel Stapleton of Reed Elsevier was reported to have received a total pay of £571,600; David Reid of Tesco received £548,000.

Total remuneration for the best paid CFO in the US, according to *Global Finance* (July 1997), rose an astounding 97.1 per cent to an average of $2.99 million from 1995 to 1996. Rollin M. Dick of Conesco and Lennert J. Leader of American Online, to give but two examples, received a total remuneration of $12 841 150 and $10 205 240 respectively.

These people are a new breed of factor of production!

VERDICT

The world of business has changed and continues to change dramatically. Classical categorization of the factors of production – land, labour, capital, enterprise – has become redundant. In reclassifying the factors of production one has to consider the transformation of businesses that is taking place in the economy today, the nature of employment, the new breed of 'employees' in the form of chief executive officers (CEOs) and chief financial officers (CFOs) who command very high total remuneration and their efforts to enhance shareholder value, the attitude of new generation employees and the introduction of alternative methods of work.

It is not simply a question of substituting technology for labour, but the changes have brought about a transformation in the concept of 'labour' as a factor of production as perceived by neo-classical economists.

The factors of production in the new economy can be categorized as *organizational competence, customers and knowledge.*

CORE COMPETENCE AS A FACTOR OF PRODUCTION

How do companies like Sony, Honda, Sharp, Hewlett Packard and Microsoft succeed with relatively fewer resources than their competitors? The answer lies in the core competence of organizations. C. K. Prahalad and Gary Hamel, in their influential article, 'The core competence of the corporation', have generated a new school of economic thought called 'The Resource-based View of the Firm'. Prahalad and Hamel (1990) write:

> The most powerful way to prevail in global competition is still invisible to many companies. During the 1980s, top executives were judged on their ability to restructure, declutter and delayer their corporations. In the 1990s, they'll be judged on their ability to identify, cultivate, and exploit the core competencies that make growth possible – indeed, they'll have to rethink the concept of the corporation itself.
>
> Consider the last ten years of GTE and NEC. In the early 1980s, GTE was well positioned to become a major player in the evolving information technology industry. It was active in telecommunications. Its operations spanned a variety of businesses including telephones, switching and transmission systems, digital PABX, semiconductors, packet switching, satellites, defence systems, and lighting products. And GTE's Entertainment Products Group, which produced Sylvania colour TVs, had a position in related display technologies. In 1980 GTE's sales were $49.98 billion, and net cash flow was $1.73 billion. NEC, in contrast, was much smaller, at $3.8 billion in sales. It had a comparable technological base and computer businesses, but it had no experience as an operating telecommunications company.
>
> Yet look at the positions of GTE and NEC in 1988. GTE's 1988 sales were $16.46 billion, and NEC's sales were considerably higher at $421.89 billion. GTE has, in effect, become a telephone operating company with a position in defence and lighting products. GTE's other businesses are small in global terms. GTE has divested Sylvania TV and Telenet, put switching, transmission, and digital PABX into joint ventures, and closed

down semiconductors. As a result, the international position of GTE has eroded. Non-US revenue as a percent of total revenue dropped from 20% to 15% between 1980 and 1988.

NEC has emerged as the world leader in semiconductors and as a first-tier player in telecommunications products and computers. It has moved beyond public switching and transmission to include such lifestyle products as mobile telephones, facsimile machines, and laptop computers – bridging the gap between telecommunications and office automation. NEC is the only company in the world to be in the top five in revenue in telecommunications, semiconductors, and mainframes. Why did these two companies, starting with comparable business portfolios, perform so differently? Largely because NEC conceived of itself in terms of 'core competencies' and GTE did not.

In the short run, a company's competitiveness derives from the price/performance attributes of current products. But the survivors of the first wave of global competition, Western and Japanese alike, are all converging on similar and formidable standards for product cost and quality – minimum hurdles for continued competition, but less and less important as sources of differential advantage. In the long run, competitiveness derives from an ability to build, at lower cost and more speedily than competitors, the core competencies that spawn unanticipated products. The real sources of advantage are to be found in management's ability to consolidate corporatewide technologies and production skills into competencies that empower individual businesses to adapt quickly to changing opportunities.

The diversified corporation is a large tree. The trunk and major limbs are core products; the smaller branches are business units; the leaves, flowers, and fruit are end products. The root system that provides nourishment, sustenance, and stability is the core competence. You can miss the strength of competitors by looking only at their end products, in the same way you miss the strength of a tree if you look only at the leaves.

Core competencies are the collective learning in the organisation, especially how to co-ordinate diverse production skills and integrate multiple teams of technologies . . . Core competence is communication, involvement, and deep commitment to working across organisational boundaries. It involves many levels of people and all functions . . . core competence does not diminish with use. Unlike physical assets, which do deteriorate over time, competencies are enhanced as they are applied and shared. But competencies still need to be nurtured and protected; knowledge fades if it is not used. Competencies are the glue that binds existing businesses. They are also the engine of new business development. Patterns of diversification and market entry may be guided by them, not just by the attractiveness of markets.

. . . We believe an obsession with competence building will characterise the global winners of the 1990s. With the decade underway the time for rethinking the concept of the corporation is already overdue.

This article has generated a lot of debate over the years since it was published in 1990. According to Dr Mansour Javidan, Professor of Strategic Management at the University of Calgary, Canada, two important questions need further work and elaboration they are: 'How do we define core competencies and capabilities?' and 'How should a corporation identify its core competencies and their implications?'

In his article 'Core Competence: What Does it Mean in Practice?', Professor Javidan (1998) explains the nature of core competencies. He highlights the existence of a hierarachy of a competencies in an organization.

Javidan says an organization has a range of resources. To what extent these resources are used effectively will depend on the ability of the organization in question. If it has the ability to use the resources effectively, then that reflects the organization's capability. Again, there may exist a range of organizational capabilities. The capabilities are essentially functionally based representing different functions of an organization, for example marketing, finance, manufacturing etc. Coordination of a range of capabilities is brought about by competency. When such co-ordination is done at department or business unit level, then that reflects the competency of that department or unit. Accordingly, an organization will have a range of competencies.

Core competence is the ability to co-ordinate all competencies. It embodies skills and knowledge that cut across all business units.

Competence and business strategy

For competence to act as a factor of production, it has to drive an organization's strategy and make things happen for that organization.

> **For competence to act as a factor of production, it has to drive an organization's strategy and make things happen for that organization**

How should organizations formulate competence strategy? Good guidelines are provided by Professor Kjell Gronhaug and Professor Odd Nordhaug (1992), both of the Norwegian School of Economics and Business Administration, in their article ' Strategy and Competence in Firms'. In relation to competence strategy they write:

In the strategic management literature, a distinction is drawn between the formulation and implementation of corporate strategy. A common point of departure for strategy formulation is analyses of external factors and in-house conditions. Next, a strategy (solution) is sought which aims at utilising the organisation's skills and other resources in the best possible way. The implementation phase involves executing the strategy that has been formulated. A stepwise approach may hence be used when competence is considered in the context of strategy development This is illustrated in Fig. 6.1.

1. The estimation step has much in common with so-called external analysis in strategic management. Estimating the competence requirement is often very complex and requires a considerable amount of relevant and accurate information. The point of departure is an assessment of opportunities and threats in the market, as represented by customer demand and competitors' offerings. This requires an understanding or a mapping of the

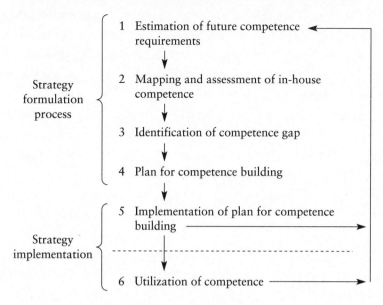

Fig. 6.1 Competence strategy: stepwise approach

products and services the market demands – and the type of competence needed by the firm in order to meet those demands. In some situations, the requirements are explicitly stated. For example, in order to become a supplier to the large oil companies operating offshore in the Norwegian part of the North sea, it is first necessary to be granted admission to a so-called bidders list. The requirements are specified in detail, and potential suppliers must document that these requirements can be met. In this context, the customers deliver accurate specifications of what they want, which makes it much easier for potential suppliers to estimate the competences needed to meet their demands. In other cases, however, estimating the required competence will be considered difficult. The competence requirement must then be derived from the type of products or services the firm wants to offer on the market, its strategy, and how this is implemented. A firm that decides to shift its first priority from growth to profitability may, for example, uncover needs for tighter economic control and management and this may in turn lead to the detection of competence requirements in the areas of accounting, business economics, cost control, internal auditing, and computer technology.

2. The second step involves mapping and assessing existing competences within the firm. It is usually easy to register the amount and substance of formal competence, because it is clearly documented. To map and assess each individual's actual competence is far more difficult. Many individual competences may not be known at all. Mapping of such latent competences will, when possible to accomplish, lay bare a discrepancy between actual and realised competence. This type of analysis will be useful for many organisations as it may uncover valuable competences which are not currently being utilised but that can be useful for the organisation if applied.

3. Through a comparison of the competence requirements and existing in-house competence, missing competence, *the competence gap*, is identified. It may turn out that the organisation, without having been aware of this, already possesses the required competence. If this is not the case, a plan for acquisition and development of necessary competence has to be elaborated.

4. The competence building plan aims at closing the estimated competence gap and may include many different development activities. Training is among the most important, embracing formal training through educational programmes and courses carried out either in-house or by external agencies. Informal learning in the workplace, such as on-the job training, is not less important, although it may be more difficult to register and govern. Recruitment is another major element in competence building plans, the importance of which will increase in most industrialised countries due to the smaller young cohorts that will enter the labour market in the decade ahead. Career planning represents a third type of relevant activity. Here the goal is to activate and develop competence in-house through the joint planning of internal job mobility and competence development. In addition, competence can be hired on a temporary basis . . . Finally, forming alliances or merging with other companies are possible avenues of strengthening the firm's competence base . . .

5. The implementation of the competence building plan is a critical phase. In-house development activities must be designed, organised, and pursued. When external sources of development are employed, needs must be clearly communicated and the outcomes of the development process adapted to the needs of the organisation. It is, moreover, crucial

for the prospects of success that the need for increased competence is communicated to employees and, moreover, they are motivated and ready to accomplish the necessary competence development. In organisations relying heavily on teamwork, it is crucial also to develop co-operative team competences as a part of the competence building plan.

6. The first four steps in Fig. 6.1 correspond to the strategy formulation process. In other words, they relate to decisions about the types of competence needed by the organisation and how these can be generated. The last two steps are linked to the strategy implementation process. Here, the utilisation of competence, which is necessary in order to maintain and further develop the organisational competence, is also included. If competence is not being applied, it is of little value and may easily deteriorate. Conversely, when competences are frequently used, they often increase in value because they are improved through practice. The feedback arrows in Fig. 6.1 indicate that through the development and utilisation of competence, the organisation may become aware of other weaknesses in its competence base and opportunities that will require new or modified competence.

Concluding comments

The significance of competences as productive resources in firms is increasing as the possession of the right competences becomes even more crucial for their future performance. This puts emphasis on establishing a good match between competences, and especially the core competence on the one hand and the strategy of the firm on the other. Concurrently, the competences must contribute to the creation of flexibility by being extensible to alternative business applications, hence facilitating strategic change if required.

As the opportunities of achieving and maintaining enduring technological leadership are diminishing in most industries, the firm's capacity to retain, develop, organise and utilise the competences will be at the forefront when its future success is to be determined . . .

Source: Reprinted from Kjell Gronhaug and Odd Nordhaug, 'Strategy and competence in firms', *European Management Journal*, Number 4, December, 1992, pp. 441–442, with permission from Elsevier Science.

Competencies provide capabilities to organizations to become 'fast, flexible and focused'. Competencies, therefore, constitute a distinct group of factors of production. As such in practice it is important for businesses to identify such competencies. Gronhaug and Nordhaug present a schematic way of identifying competencies for businesses.

Core competencies and service firms

Jacques Horovitz (1997) argues that the concept of core competencies applies to service organizations as well. He writes:

> It is also possible in the service industry to create new business opportunities by transferring competencies from one business to another as Canon did when in 1976, it utilised the competencies in optics and imaging for the AE1 camera to introduce the first personal copier and surpass Xerox market share by 1983.
>
> Today services account for more than 70 per cent of employment and GNP. Many industrial corporations also owe their revenue and profitability to the peripheral services that add on to their products. This makes the issue both relevant and important. For example, what are the chances of IBM succeeding in its move towards the service sector if the required core competencies differ from those in research or production or if they cannot be transferred? How does the service corporation choose to diversify in order to benefit from its know-how? Is the development of the service company into a new unrelated sector ever possible?
>
> In order to discover those competencies that can be used in development for the service industry, let us consider the case of corporations that have never manufactured any products.
>
> Générale des Eaux (GdE) – one of the biggest European players in water supply – participates today in a variety of businesses such as water, hospitals and security. The group recently purchased Elitair's catering division (serving airports and in-company cafeterias). Should this move be

Competencies provide capabilities to organizations to become 'fast, flexible and focused'.

considered a diversification with no relation to GdE's existing businesses – with as few chances of success as any 'unrelated' diversification – or could it utilise its core competency in dealing with municipalities when negotiating a food service contract for a jail, school or hospital?

How could Accor be as successful in the hotel business as it is in the restaurant business? Are there common competencies? Does its recent investment in the tourism industry (the purchase of Wagon Lits travel and the merger with Carson, the US travel agency chain) call for the same competencies and know-how as with hotels and restaurants?

Why did Marriott recently separate itself from the real estate development efforts to concentrate on hotel management? Was it just a matter of finance or was it that 'wheeler dealer' know-how of real estate has difficulty marrying with the daily management of the 101 details necessary in hotel management?

Why did Club Med fail in the airline business after purchasing Minerve – an air charter company? And why is Nouvelles Frontières – another European tour operator specializing in cheap travel for young adults – successful with the airline it has purchased?

The answers to all the questions lie in identifying and deploying core competencies. Horovitz continues:

> The core competencies of service companies represent the essence of corporate know-how underlying each business. Precisely identifying them is the first step towards opening up to growth opportunities. Just because Club Med is in the travel business does not mean that the company has the appropriate know-how to manage aeroplanes, pilots, landing rights, leasing or maintenance.

Competencies matter in manufacturing as well as service sectors. Organizations need to develop their resources into capabilities and create appropriate competencies by building their capabilities.

VERDICT

Core competence in the new economy constitutes one of the factors of production. Core competence enables organizations not only to gain but also to sustain competitive advantage. Viewed from core competence perspective, organizations function like open systems. Core competence, therefore, becomes one of the key factors of production in the new economy.

CUSTOMERS AS A FACTOR OF PRODUCTION

In traditional economics an entrepreneur co-ordinates factors of production (land, labour, capital) in order to produce goods. The process of production involves the creation of utilities and the creation of value. Goods are produced to meet the needs of consumers. In a value chain concept, the factors of production create value while consumers 'destroy' value in the process of consumption.

In information age organizations, suppliers and customers are interlinked in a global business web with constantly changing relationships. Customers have become very important in driving corporate strategy and they should be considered as value creators and one of the key factors of production in the new economy. Rosabeth Moss Kanter (1989) wrote about forming alliances with customers because customers are the single best source of new business and by listening to them products and production can be aligned to their requirements. They can also become a source of ideas and

> *Customers have become very important in driving corporate strategy and they should be considered as value creators and one of the key factors of production in the new economy.*

innovation. According to one author, today customers are users, influencers, deciders, approvers, buyers and gatekeepers.

Customers as value creators

In the 1970s hardly anyone had heard of customer satisfaction, customer retention and customer loyalty. Now many organizations focus their strategies on customers as links between customer satisfaction and profitability become established and as organizations come to understand how customers can create value. Value created by customers takes a different format.

Dr. Rafael Ramirez (1999) of HEC School of Management, Paris, writes:

- If one takes customers – such as you, the reader of this paper – as creating rather than destroying value, there are significant implications in the emerging economy.
- 'Value' is not simply added but jointly invented and produced.
- 'Final' customers do not exist.
- 'Needs' are not useful in determining how to relate to customers.
- 'Value' is not 'in' the good or service but is interactively established.
- What competes in the marketplace are offerings not companies.
- The distinction between 'goods' and 'services' needs to be rethought.

Customers are becoming more informed, more educated and thus more intelligent. They should be considered as value creators. Ramirez begins:

As you read this newspaper are you creating value or destroying it?

A lot depends on how you answer this question. Your reply will align you with one or two radically different views of the economy. In the industrial economy we are now exiting, consumption of goods or services by customers was assumed to destroy the value that producers had created for them.

This view is being increasingly questioned as an alternative economy emerges. This article argues that while you use up the pulp and paper, the ink, and the intellectual and information resources that the *Financial Times* employed to produce this paper, your reading it creates value. Your reading more than compensates for the physical destruction that rumpling the paper and rubbing off the ink contributes to.

In the same way, all customers in the emerging economy need to be considered as value creators for business.

Customers also create value for businesses in a different way. The following are snapshots of how customers influence the way organizations conduct their businesses.

Customers and ABB

Customers have, since the 1980s, become the focus of business strategy. Asea Brown Boveri's (ABB) core businesses are power generation, power transmission and distribution, industrial automation and transportation. The strength of the group lies in the flexibility of belonging to a big organization. They started their customer focus initiative in 1990. The approach they adopted had the following key elements:

- Continuous improvement of performance and process shall be based on an interaction between time-based management, total quality management and supply management;
- the result shall exceed the expectations of the customer and support ABB goals;
- the approach shall be a substantial part of the strategy and completely integrated in all issues.

The organization now has customer focus groups consisting of panels of customers who give feedback on products and competition. Senior managers in some companies visit customers taking cross-functional groups with them. Businesses send questionnaires and commission various customer surveys in order to 'get close to their customers'.

Comments

ABB has become a well-known company because it has managed change over the years very effectively. It has decentralized its structure to get close to customers. It has made customer satisfaction the cornerstone of its business strategy.

Customers and DHL

DHL International (UK) until very recently, was a functionally driven organization where any given station or office would have someone responsible for managing the operations – the couriers, sorting and so on – and someone else responsible for managing sales. They did away with this structure and created mini-businesses at the lowest possible level in order to take decision making closer to the customers. This resulted in the creation of station managers who in turn reported to station directors.

DHL also used market research to gain in-depth knowledge of their customers' wants. They built up the following hierarchy of needs and wants based on the information received:

Fundamental factors
- service reliability
- on-time delivery
- security handling
- worldwide delivery.

Efficacy factors
- pricing/tariff
- tracking and tracing
- documentation
- pick-up/application.

Added value factors
- personnel relationships
- business partner.

They instituted a 'cradle to grave' relationship with their customers. This policy is an approach to communication planning which is responsive to the current requirements and potential of customers as their relationship grows with a supplier. The 'cradle to grave' policy establishes exactly where in the customer lifecycle DHL are currently sitting so they can tailor their communication precisely to address that position.

There are two sides to the business equation: costs and revenues. In economics, the focus has been on marginal cost and marginal revenue in terms of maximizing profit. In relation to the factors of production the emphasis has been on costs – determining wages, interest, rent and profit. Modern businesses have shifted the emphasis to costs in terms of restructuring, process reengineering and cost-reduction strategies and to revenues in terms of winning and retaining customers. Customers now play a key role in driving organizational transformation and in influencing the way products and services are delivered.

These organizations which enter for the Malcolm Baldridge National Quality Award in the US have to score 250 out of 1000 points for 'customer focus and satisfaction'. The customer category involves elements like determining customer requirements and expectations; customer relationship management; customer service standards; commitment to customers; complaint resolution for quality improvement; determining customer satisfaction; customer satisfaction results and customer satisfaction comparison which involves comparisons with competitors.

> *Customers now play a key role in driving organizational transformation and in influencing the way products and services are delivered.*

As far as the European Quality award is concerned the 'customer satisfaction' category carries 200 out of 1000 points. A customer is defined as the immediate customer of the organization and all other customers in the complete chain of distribution of its products and services. Organizations are assessed on various elements including the capability of meeting product and service specifications; delivery performance; sales and technical support; responsiveness and flexibility in meeting customer needs; value for money; measuring repeat, new and lost business; defect, error and rejection rates; complaints profiling and handling and so on.

Comments

DHL face fierce competition from United Parcel service (UPS) and Federal Express, not to mention other national and international courier companies. Listening to their customers enabled DHL to rationalize their operations and reduce bureaucratic organizational structure.

Customers and British Airways

In an interview with British Airways' Sir Colin Marshall (Prokesch, 1995), when answering a question on different ways of competing, said:

> There's another critical element of our approach to serving customers: Fulfilling customers' value-driven needs. Every industry has a price of entry – the ante you have to pay to get into the game. In our industry, there are five basic services that everyone has to provide. We must get passengers to where they want to go, do it safely, go when they want to go, provide some nourishment and let them accrue frequent-flier miles. But our research shows that customers now take the basics for granted and increasingly want a company to desire to help them, to treat them in a personal, caring way. Fulfilling those desires is the centrepiece of how we wish to orchestrate our service.

When asked what he meant by orchestrating service, he replied:

> We try to think about what kind of impression or feeling each interaction between the company and a customer will generate . . . We continually ask

customers in focus groups to tell us what such an experience should look and feel like, and we have distilled their responses into service principles that are enshrined in two of our corporate goals. The goals are: 'To provide overall superior service and good value for money in every market segment in which we compete' and 'to excel in anticipating and quickly responding to customer needs and competitor activity'. These corporate goals have, in turn, been incorporated into our customer service department's mission statement: 'To ensure that British Airways is the customer's first choice through the delivery of an unbeatable travel experience.'

On replying to the question of how British Airways expect to fulfil customers' value-driven needs, he said:

> By creating an organization that excels in listening to its most valuable customers. By creating data that enable you to measure the kinds of performance that creates value for those customers so you can improve performance and spot and correct any weaknesses. And by recognising that the people on the front line are the ones who ultimately create value since they are the ones who determine the kinds of experiences that the company generates for its customers. We focus intensively on the customer, and our marketing, our operating philosophy and our performance measures reflect that.
>
> Source: Reprinted by permission of *Harvard Business Review*. From Steven E. Prokesch, 'Competing on customer service: an interview with British Airways' Sir Colin Marshall', *Harvard Business Review*, November–December, 1995, pp. 103–106. Copyright 1995 by the President and Fellows of Harvard College; all rights reserved.

Comments

British Airways were forced to rethink how they managed their customer interface in order to retain their competitive advantage.

Customers and TNT

TNT's culture is focused implicitly and explicitly on anticipating and serving customer needs. Traditional transport businesses place great emphasis on the hardware – depots, trucks, warehouses – and shaping rosters. TNT resolutely styles itself as a service business, run by people to serve people. Although the company demonstrates innovative use of technology to solve complex logistical problems, hardware is there solely to facilitate the job of satisfying customers and doing so more cost efficiently than competitors.

The transport and distribution business has been subject to constant change over the past 10 years. TNT has flourished and relished the challenge, and in many cases has been the agent of change. Numerous breakthrough improvements include the introduction of hub and spoke distribution, the first UK next-day guaranteed door to door delivery service, the unique Sameday Service and computerised sortation systems. These have, arguably, changed the face of the whole industry. In our areas, the company has responded to specific customer needs and changed the face of the businesses. Ten years ago, most UK national newspapers were carried by rail. Now most travel by road, and largely by TNT.

Source: *European Quality Award Special Report*, 1995, European Quality Publications Ltd. London. pp. 62–64. Reprinted with permission.

Comments

In the case of TNT the focus of attention was put on improving logistics to meet customer needs. They improved their delivery time in order to remain ahead of the game. Customer needs changed the whole nature of the distribution industry.

Customers and Orange plc

Philip Hendey (1997), Head of Relationship Management at Orange writes:

Orange has always put a great deal of emphasis on customer service. It was awarded the Best Customer Service Award from industry publication *Mobile News* earlier this year (1997). To support our commitment to customer service, Orange runs customer retention and development programmes that extend Orange's reputation of value for money and quality service. One of the most visible of these is a customer programme we called Horizons, which allows customers to buy goods from third parties at special rates, using their Orange phone.

Every Orange customer automatically becomes a member. Focus group interviews to find out how many Orange customers knew about the programme revealed 92% recall. A number of those interviewed even pulled out their Horizons membership cards. According to our research, the percentage of Orange customers taking advantage of Horizons offers is up to 10% of our customer base.

So Horizons is beginning to provide benefits to Orange customers. But what benefits accrue to 'Orange' from Horizons? Firstly, the fact that the customer has to use their Orange phone to make their call to Horizons thereby encouraging further familiarity with the phone and building revenue. To make Horizons cost-effective, Orange had to strike deals with third parties to make the offers available. These deals have the added advantage that they extend the Orange brand into other areas of customers' life; for instance, they associate a good bottle of wine with the Orange brand.

Information about Orange customer purchases also gives Orange the opportunity to develop offerings it knows its customers want. In addition, Orange has just launched a new membership scheme, called Equity, that will aim to reinforce the benefits of being an Orange customer. It rewards customers for items such as their phone usage and talk plan selection. These rewards then give customers access to accessories, merchandise or, for example, cinema tickets. In addition, last year Orange and NatWest joined forces to launch the Orange Visa card, which offered a competitive financial package and added further value to customers.

Source: Philip Hendey, 'How Orange, part of the global Hutchison Whampoa empire, broke the mould of the UK's mobile phone industry by putting the customer first', *Customer Service Management*, September, 1997, pp. 14–17. Reprinted with permission.

Comments

Orange's strategy revolved around customer retention and rewarding customer loyalty. All the above cases show how customer needs and satisfaction drive business strategy irrespective of whether you are in transport, telecommunications or distribution sectors. The concept of 'consumer sovereignty' has been transformed into 'customer sovereignty'.

VERDICT

In traditional economics, economists did emphasize the importance of consumers by putting forward the theory of marginal diminishing utility and the concept of demand and scale of preference. In new economics the attention has shifted to customers, the decision-makers.

So far in this book examples have been provided of a small range of organizations which are influenced and driven by customers' needs to be satisfied, thus shaping the way organizations do their business today. Customers will increasingly become a key factor of production, especially as we travel down the road of this information age.

EXECUTIVE SUMMARY

- In traditional economics land, labour, capital and enterprise constitute the factors of production. These factors are inputs in a supply chain which produces goods and services. They have remained at the centre of economics despite various changes that are taking place in the business world.

- The changes in the business world affect the way people work, the way they perceive their work, the way they are organized, the way organizations are configuring themselves to remain competitive and the way technology is used to underpin corporate strategies.

- New breeds of 'entrepreneurs' are developing within the corporate world whose rewards bear no resemblance to the rewards based on the principle of marginal productivity.

- In 'new economics' the core competence of an organization constitutes one of the three key factors of production, the other two being customers and knowledge (see Gateway Seven).

- Core competence has to be identified and utilized effectively. Explanations and guidelines are provided to enable an organization to identify and utilize its core competence in order to gain and maintain competitive advantage.

- The second key factor of production in new economics is the customer. Many organizations are formulating their strategies to focus their attention on getting close to the customer.

- Examples are given on how companies like ABB, DHL, British Airways, TNT and Orange focus their attention on their customers.

- Customers add as well as create value in a supply chain.

References

Apgar, Mahlon (1998) 'The alternative workplace: changing where and how people work', *Harvard Business Review*, May–June, 128.

European Quality Award Special Report (1995) London: European Quality Publications.

Global Finance (1996), '£636,000' September, 15.

Gronhaug, Kjell and Nordhaug, Odd (1992) 'Strategy and competence in firms', *European Management Journal*, 4, December, 441–2.

Handy, Charles (1995) *Beyond Certainty: The Changing Worlds of Organisations.* London: Hutchinson.

Hendey, Philip (1997) 'How Orange, part of the Global Hutchison Whampoa empire, broke the mould of the UK's mobile phone industry by putting the customer first', *Customer Service Management*, September 14–17.

Horovitz, Jacques (1997) 'Core competencies and service firms' in *FT Mastering Management*. London: Financial Times Management, 583–5.

Javidan, Mansour (1998) 'Core competence: what does it mean in practice?', *Long Range Planning*, 31: 1, 60–71.

Kahn, Sheraton (1997) 'Zoom', *Global Finance*, July, 23.

Moss Kanter, Rosabeth (1983) *The Change Masters – Corporate Entrepreneurs at Work*. London: Unwin.

Moss Kanter, Rosabeth (1989) *When Giants Learn to Dance*. New York: Simon & Schuster.

Prahalad, C.K. and Hamel, Gary (1990) 'The core competence of the corporation', *Harvard Business Review*, May–June, 79–82.

Prokesch, Steven E. (1995) 'Competing on customer service: an interview with British Airway's Sir Colin Marshall', *Harvard Business Review*, November–December, 103–6.

Ramirez, Rafael (1999) 'Unchaining value in a new economic age' in *FT Mastering Global Business*. London: Financial Times Management, 129–32.

NEW PERSPECTIVES ON THE FACTORS OF PRODUCTION II
Knowledge

The chief economic *priority for developed countries, therefore, must be to raise the productivity of knowledge and service work. The country that does this first will dominate the twenty-first century.*

Peter Drucker

The dominant competitive weapon of the twenty-first century will be the education and skills of the workforce.
Lester Thurow

INTRODUCTION

Knowledge as such is an appreciating asset; the more it is used the more effective its application. It is said that information added with the addition of intelligence transforms into knowledge and that knowledge with the addition of imagination becomes innovation.

In a modern business context organizations have to come up with innovative strategies and structures in order to compete effectively in a global arena. They have technology as an enabler but the winners would be those companies who learn to harness knowledge within their organizations and become industrial leaders.

KNOWLEDGE AND INCREASING RETURNS

Knowledge is presented as the third and last factor of production in the new economy. Knowledge, unlike land, labour and capital, is an appreciating asset. The more it is used the more effective it becomes. *It incorporates the principle of increasing returns.* This also means that knowledge is an infinite resource which an organization has at its disposal. According to Karl Erick Sveiby knowledge has four characteristics. It is tacit, action-oriented, supported by rules, and is constantly changing. The creation, acquisition and effective deployment of knowledge in an organization has become the key source of competitive advantage.

A *McKinsey Quarterly* editorial (1998) highlights the following characteristics of knowledge:

- extraordinary leverage and increasing returns – once knowledge has been created the initial development cost can be spread over increasing volumes
- fragmentation, leakage and need for refreshment
- uncertain value – value is often difficult to estimate
- uncertain value-sharing.

The nature and uses of knowledge

A special issue of *European Management Journal* on managing knowledge and intellectual capital was published in August 1996. The following two extracts are presented from a variety of articles which explain the nature of knowledge, the importance of knowledge in an organization, and how it is used to create competitive advantage. The second extract will be presented in the form of a case study.

> *The creation, acquisition and effective deployment of knowledge in an organization has become the key source of competitive advantage.*

The first extract by Leif Edvinson, Vice President and Director, Intellectual Capital at Skandia Assurance, Stockholm and Patrick Sullivan (1996), President of a consulting organization.

THE KNOWLEDGE FIRM

Companies that use their knowledge as a source of competitive advantage are called 'knowledge companies'. Knowledge companies derive their profits from the commercialisation of the knowledge created by their human resource – their employees. In some cases, knowledge companies differentiate themselves from the competition through their knowledge. Knowledge companies are found in value-adding industries. In the product field they include computer companies and other high-tech firms, software companies, and manufacturers of new or differentiated products. Knowledge companies in the services industry include law firms, consulting firms, financial services firms, and media companies (newspaper, periodicals, television, and radio).

Knowledge companies in contrast with smokestack companies, leverage newly defined kinds of capital: intellectual and structural. Both of these new kinds of assets have as their basis the human resource, the most fundamental element to the firm's revenue-generating capability. All firms have structural capital – it includes all of the firm's tangible balance-sheet assets. These assets include the infrastructure that provides support for the firm's intellectual capital as well as for the firm's complementary business assets so necessary to maximising profits for the firm. But for knowledge companies, it is the structural capital that provides the most valuable and leveraged asset.

Knowledge

A discussion of intellectual capital is best understood if one has a clear understanding of 'knowledge' in the business context. Business knowledge generally is of two kinds: that which is codified and that which is tacit. This distinction is very important strategically. Knowledge is definable and can be protected by the legal system, whether as trade secrets, patents, copyrights, or semiconductor masks. If not protected by intellectual property law, codified information is often easy to imitate. In contrast, tacit knowledge, or know-how, is by nature difficult to describe. It can be demonstrated but rarely codified. Tacit knowledge gets transferred through demonstration and on-the-job training. Process knowledge, in manufacturing firms in particular, is often tacit. Relationship knowledge, often found in service firms, is also usually tacit. As with many things, the tacit knowledge position can be both an advantage and a disadvantage. Because it is difficult to transfer, tacit know-how is inherently protected. Once transferred, however, there are few means for the original owner to re-assert ownership.

Three other dimensions of knowledge are worth mentioning. The first is whether it is visualised in use or not. Some knowledge can be commercialised without being observed by others. Process knowledge is often of that kind. Product knowledge is different; to sell it, you have to reveal it to others. A second dimension of note is the complexity or simplicity of the knowledge. And third, we must note whether knowledge can stand alone, or whether it has value only when embedded in some kind of integrated system. Whether knowledge is autonomous affects the way you manage its commercialisation.

Knowledge companies have been defined earlier to be those using the knowledge as a source of competitive advantage; an intellectual capital for those firms is 'knowledge that can be converted into value'. How do knowledge firms create value from their intellectual capital?

There are two fundamental sources of value inherent in the knowledge firm model. The first is the innovations themselves. Commercialisable innovations are generated by the firm's human resource, converted into intellectual assets, and legally protected. These innovations become the fuel that drives the firm's business engine. Firms can have too many innovations just as they can have too few. For firms having too many innovations, their management must develop methods of screening out the less desirable innovations and identifying those that will generate the most value for the firm. Conversely, firms with too few innovations must develop processes that will stimulate innovation (particularly in certain technologies or innovation areas of importance to the firm).

The second source of value for knowledge companies resides in the conversion by a firm's structural business assets. These assets (e.g., processing, distribution, sales) add value to the innovation as it is converted from an intangible into a product or service for which customers will pay. In terms of extracting value for business assets, knowledge firms are no different than others, they are able to achieve revenue from the value added by each structural business asset during the process of converting an innovation from an intangible into a saleable item.

Source: Reprinted from Leif Edvinson and Patrick Sullivan, 'Developing a model for managing intellectual capital', *European Management Journal*, Volume 14, August, 1996, pp. 357–8, with permission from Elsevier Science.

Knowledge in the form of intellectual property or capital has replaced labour and capital as a factor of production. Many organizations do not make effective use of knowledge to create wealth. The authors of the above article explore different dimensions of knowledge and their uses in practice. It is important to identify tacit knowledge and to have a strategy to use it effectively.

The second extract is by Ann B. Graham, contributing editor of The Economist Intelligence Unit, and Vincent Pizzo (1996) of IBM Consulting Group, New York.

> *Knowledge in the form of intellectual property or capital has replaced labour and capital as a factor of production.*

Case study

3M: 'THOU SHALT NOT KILL IDEAS'

The Economist has called 3M's balancing approach 'conservatism with creativity'. CEO Livio DeSimone characterises it as 'innovation and stability'. While learning values keep 3M's inventors on the creative edge, management is vigilant about linking continuous learning and innovation to revenues. A well-known corporate target demands that 30 per cent of 3M's annual sales come from products less than four years old. Compensation for senior and division managers is also tied to the percentage of sales from new products. Other aggressive annual financial goals include 10 per cent growth in earnings per share, 27 per cent return on capital employed and an 8 per cent rise in sales per employee. Beyond the discipline of financial measures, 3M's creativity and productivity is sustained by the firm's institutional management of two key knowledge areas: (1) core technology competencies that keep the new product pipeline full and diverse; (2) corporate values that honour the needs of the innovators.

At the heart of the innovation process is the notion that 3M's 60,000 products belong to business sectors, groups, and divisions. Technology, however, belongs to the company. Approximately 33 technologies (e.g., adhesives, and microreplication) are organised in 'platforms' that generate 'multiple products for multiple markets'. Platforms are represented in product portfolios across the company . . .

▶

With centralised 'ownership' of the core technologies, 3M promotes knowledge transfer and entrepreneurial management unmatched among most firms its size. More than 8,000 scientists and researchers in over 100 laboratories work together without the secrecy typical of the not-invented-here syndrome. Scientists have always encouraged colleagues to try out their discoveries. Today, a vast computerised database allows scientists to share their enterprise more systematically and enables other employees to easily connect with the technology experts. Cross-fertilisation of ideas and technology is also facilitated through two institutional groups that support personal networking among scientists.

On the cultural side, values captured in corporate maxims and stories express unusual support for individual creativity. The phrase 'grow and divide' describes how 3M has been able to retain the entrepreneurialism that is often lost in large organisations by encouraging employees to develop their product ideas in small, dynamic teams. Indeed many of 3M's most lucrative profit centres began as project teams consisting of an individual with an idea and a few supporters. If the divisions grow large enough, they may break apart again to restore the dynamism.

The sanctity of time is embodied in the infamous '15 per cent rule', which requires all employees to set aside 15 per cent of their work time to pursue personal research interests. Another familiar 3M homily, 'Thou shall not kill new ideas for products' is known as the 11th commandment. It is the source of countless stories, including the one that tells how Mr DeSimone tried five times (and failed) to kill the project that yielded the 3M blockbuster, Thinsulate™.

3M's corporate language and story telling traditions are part of training programmes that teach newcomers and remind old timers about unwritten rules and informal ways work actually gets done. For instance, the 11th commandment reinforces the acceptance of challenging superiors or the patience required to shepherd projects for years before they yield results.

Leaders in the company see themselves as the keepers of the values.

Mr DeSimone says, 'the primary role of senior management is to create an internal environment in which people understand and value our way of operating'. More specifically he says, 'Our job is one of creation and destruction – supporting individual initiative while breaking down bureaucracy and cynicism. It all depends on developing a personal trust relationship between those at the top and the lower levels.' (Bartlett and Goshal, 1995)

In addition to its corporate financial measures, 3M's conservatism emerges in rigorous checks and balances in the project development and funding systems. For example, once a product development team receives its first round of funding, it must meet clear objectives and be able to market its ideas to coaches and supporters in management to qualify for the next round. And while project champions do not need top brass approval to get started, when the costs or market potential are high, the project must pass the toughest security of 3M's top executives. Another mechanism, 'pacing programs', selects high potential projects for accelerated funding. For instance, Apex, an abrasive material made from a microreplication application, was evolving slowly on a researcher's 15 per cent time, until it was recognised as a potential half billion dollar business. A 'pacing program' accelerated the Apex launch from 1998 to 1995.

At a time when many companies have underestimated the downside of downsizing for morale, 3M has stood by its belief that knowledge is best cultivated through personal loyalty and trust built through long-term associations. Until recently, the company resisted layoffs due to business fluctuations; employee turnover has historically been limited to about 3 per cent a year. However, in the face of today's competitive pressures, even 3M is questioning whether it can sustain their record. That it may no longer be able to do so was implied in the 1995 re-organisation announcement that will require a workforce reduction of 5,000 jobs, at least 1,000 of which may be layoffs.

Source: Reprinted from Ann Graham and Vincent Pizzo, 'A question of balance: strategic knowledge management', *European Management Journal*, Volume 14, August 1996, p. 338 with permission from Elsevier Science.

The success of 3M is based on continuous innovation. They have cultivated and used knowledge very effectively within their organization.

Following 3M's story, it is evident that the role of entrepreneurship and knowledge becomes significant in the new information age economics of the firm. In the article 'The New Economics of Organization', which is based on a McKinsey research programme, Jonathan D. Day and James C. Wendler (1998) write:

> Organisations exist to motivate their members and co-ordinate their activities. In general, corporate performance suffers when there is a lack of motivation, coordination, or both.
>
> For many companies, the chief challenge is insufficient *entrepreneurialism:* a failure to motivate top talent to seize opportunities and make the most of them. For others, the problem is an inability to develop, apply, and capture value from new technologies and practices, and to forge value-creating linkages between processes, business units, and core functions. We might think of this as primarily a *knowledge* challenge, or lack of coordination.
>
> Many of the greatest challenges a corporation faces in coordinating its activities relate to knowledge. Though it pervades all forms of activity, knowledge has received surprisingly little management attention outside technical contexts. It must now become a central managerial concern.
>
> It is easy to forget that finance made a similar transition not so long ago, spurred in part by the work of James O. McKinsey on planning and budgeting* and culminating in the development of modern corporate finance over the past 40 years. The theoretical and practical tools on which we now rely, such as net present value and the capital assets pricing

---

* A number of economists and management thinkers have pointed out the similarities between many large corporations and socialist economies. Both feature centralised asset ownership; both are characterised by vertical information flows and central planning instead of the decentralised decision making, horizontal information flows, and price-guided co-ordination mechanisms of markets. Both suffer from what economists call 'bounded rationality', or managers' inability to play the role of rational economic agents perfectly due to the limitations of the human intellect. Jay W. Forrester, founder of the system dynamics movement, develops this theme in his interview with Mark Keough and Andrew Doman, 'The CEO as organization designer.' *The McKinsey Quarterly*, 1992, Number 2, pp. 3–30.

model, were simply not available to previous generations of managers. We must learn to manage knowledge in an equally explicit and integrated way, and for the same reason: there is economic value in doing so.

Many management writers have recognised the importance of intangible assets in general, and knowledge in particular. Few managers today would confine themselves to an accountant's analysis of physical and financial assets in seeking to understand the value of a company. Yet despite the mounting interest in intellectual capital, the experience of many corporations in managing knowledge and converting it into economic value is patchy and disappointing.

Some companies have set up business units in order to boost initiative, but have then struggled to bring about the interaction between units on which knowledge generation and value creation depend. Others remain insular, even though alliances are a powerful vehicle for value creation in their industries. Still others lack the leverage and skills to capture an adequate share of the value that their alliances create. Many lack both the incentives and the resources – people, processes, systems, and knowledge itself – to generate, refresh, and share knowledge.

A knowledge-based company can inject entrepreneurialism into an organization to motivate top management staff and it can enable an organization to capture, apply and develop value from technologies.

For yet others, the knowledge challenge is more operational than strategic. An inability to share knowledge effectively means that though one business unit is aware of an opportunity, others are not, and the moment is lost. When the frontline executive is the problem, an otherwise impressive knowledge advantage fails to translate into a competitive difference.

Whereas a corporation confronting an entrepreneurialism challenge typically knows where the opportunities lie but cannot motivate its people to pursue them vigorously enough, a corporation with a knowledge challenge can be blindsided by competitors exploiting opportunities of which it is not even aware. It may simply miss the boat strategically.

To find successful organisational designs, companies must solve the challenges of entrepreneurialism and knowledge in tandem. Neither the entrepreneurial drive of talented managers nor the sophistication of knowledge-based strategies will be sufficient in itself to secure success. Tomorrow's winners must have both.

A knowledge-based company can inject entrepreneurialism into an organization to motivate top management staff and it can enable an organization to capture, apply and develop value from technologies. Organizations should learn to get maximum returns from knowledge, their intangible asset.

Case study

KNOWLEDGE MANAGEMENT AT HEWLETT-PACKARD

Knowledge management is exploding at the Hewlett-Packard Company. While there has been no stop-down mandate to manage knowledge at this highly decentralised computer and electronics manufacturer, many divisions and departments are undertaking specific efforts to do just that.

A corporate 'knowledge czar' would not fit with HP's culture, but many managers are attempting to capture and distribute the knowledge residing in their own business units and departments.

The efforts are springing up quickly, and it is difficult even to identify and track all of them. The Computer Systems Marketing organisation, for example, has put a large amount of marketing knowledge into a World Wide Web-based system that can be accessed around the world. It contains product information, competitive intelligence, white papers and ready-to-deliver marketing presentations.

HP Laboratories, meanwhile, is developing approaches to facilitate access to both internal and external knowledge. And Corporate

Information Systems is putting document-based knowledge of procedures, personnel and other information into Web and Lotus Notes systems; its manager's argue for a 'pull' approach to knowledge distribution (accessed when needed), rather than the typical 'push' strategy. Information System is also attempting to map the various sources of knowledge about information systems development and management around the company.

Perhaps the most focused, intensive approach to knowledge management is in the Product Process Organisation, or PPO, which provides the company's product divisions with such services as purchasing, engineering, market intelligence, change management and environmental and safety consulting.

Bill Kay, the director of Product Processes, believes that information and knowledge management should be a core competence, and he even put his unit's Information Systems group at the centre of the PPO organisation chart. Product Processes has adopted many approaches to knowledge transfer in the past, including catalogues of documents, video and audiotapes of meetings, best practice databases and the Work Innovation Network, a series of meetings and ongoing discussions on change management topics.

Until recently, however, there had been no formal responsibility for knowledge management in Product Processes. But in 1995, Mr. Kay formed a Knowledge Management Group within PPO's Information Systems Group. Its initial charter was to capture and leverage knowledge of the product-generation process in the various HP divisions.

The group quickly developed a prototype of a Web-based knowledge management system called Knowledge Links. Its primary content is knowledge about the product-generation process; the knowledge may come from a variety of functional perspectives, including marketing, R&D, engineering and manufacturing. The knowledge going into Knowledge Links comes from outside the Knowledge Management Group, but group members add value by identifying, editing and formatting the material, making it easier to access and use.

▶

The PPO Knowledge Management Group intends to develop a variety of other services worth broader application for PPO and for HP as a whole.

It plans to develop for internal HP clients versions of Knowledge Links for other types of knowledge. It has developed an assessment tool for weighing the levels of knowledge management capability in PPO and other company groups. It is beginning to map key knowledge domains within PPO. Finally, within the context of a Knowledge Links development activity, the group offer advice about how best to foster knowledge-creating and sharing behaviours, without which the technology is of little value.

Hewlett-Packard has been a knowledge-oriented company since its founding in 1938. Now, however, many managers throughout the company are realising that the knowledge management concept must be taken to a higher level.

Source: Davenport, Thomas 'Some Principles of Knowledge Management', *Business & Strategy*, Winter, 1996, pp. 38–9. Reprinted with permission from Booze Allen & Hamilton.

Hewlett-Packard provides a good example of how one company captures and develops knowledge in practice. It is making the most of its staff and technologies to gain value.

HOW TO MANAGE KNOWLEDGE IN BUSINESS

Professor Thomas Davenport (1996) of the University of Texas presents the following principles of knowledge management:

1   Knowledge management is expensive (but so is stupidity). Knowledge is an asset, but its effective management requires the investment of other assets, namely money and labour . . .

2   Effective management of knowledge requires hybrid solutions involving both people and technology.

    . . . People may be expensive and cantankerous, but they are quite accomplished at certain knowledge skills. When we seek to understand knowledge, to interpret it within a broader context, to combine it with other types of information or to synthesise various unstructured forms of knowledge, humans are the recommended tool.

Computers and communications systems, on the other hand, are good at capturing, transforming and distributing highly structured knowledge that changes rapidly . . .

3 Knowledge management is highly political.

It is no secret that 'knowledge is power', and thus it should not be a surprise to anyone that knowledge management is a highly political undertaking. If knowledge is associated with power, money and success, then it is also associated with lobbying, intrigue and back-room deals.

4 Knowledge management requires knowledge managers.

. . . Knowledge will not be well-managed until one group within a company has a clear responsibility for the job.

5 Knowledge management benefits more from maps than models, more from markets than hierarchies.

It is tempting when managing knowledge to create a hierarchical model of architecture, similar to the Encyclopaedia Britannica's Propaedia, that could govern collection and categorisation. But most organisations are better off letting the knowledge market work, and simply providing and mapping the knowledge that its consumers seem to want.

6 Sharing and using knowledge are often unnatural acts.

. . . We sometimes act surprised when knowledge is not shared or used, but we would be better off assuming that the natural tendency is to hoard our own knowledge and look suspiciously on knowledge that comes from others. To enter our knowledge into a system and to seek out knowledge from others is not only threatening, but also requires much effort – so we have to be highly motivated to undertake such work.

7 Knowledge management means improving knowledge work processes.

It is important to address and improve the generic knowledge management process, but knowledge is generated, used and shared intensively through specific work processes. While the details vary by company and industry, these include market research and product design and development, and even more transactional processes like order configuration and pricing. If real improvements are to be made in knowledge management, gains must occur in these key business processes.

8   Access to knowledge is only the beginning.

Access is important, but successful knowledge management also requires attention and engagement. It has been said that attention is the currency of the information age.

9   Knowledge management never ends.

One reason is that the categories of required knowledge are always changing. New technologies, management approaches, regulatory issues and customer concerns are always emerging. Companies change their strategies, organisational structures and product and service emphases. New managers and professionals have new needs for knowledge.

10   Knowledge management requires a knowledge contract.

Source: Thomas Davenport, 'Some principles of knowledge management, *Strategy & Business*, Winter, 1996, pp. 34–40. Reprinted with permission from Booze-Allen & Hamilton.

If knowledge is really becoming a more valued resource in organizations, we expect to see more attention to the legalities of knowledge management.

THE JAPANESE PERSPECTIVE ON KNOWLEDGE

Professor Ikujiro Nonaka (1991) at the Institute of Business Research and Hitotsubashi University presents a Japanese perspective:

In an economy where the only certainty is uncertainty, the one sure source of lasting competitive advantage is knowledge When markets shift, technologies proliferate, competitors multiply, and products become obsolete almost overnight, successful companies are those that consistently create knowledge, disseminate it widely throughout the organisation, and quickly embody it in new technologies and products. These activities define the 'knowledge-creating' company, whose sole business is continuous innovation.

. . . Deeply ingrained in the traditions of Western management, from Fredrick Taylor to Herbert Simon, is a view of the organisation as a machine for 'information processing'. According to this view, the only useful knowledge is formal and systematic – hard (read quantifiable) data, codified procedures, universal principles. And the key metrics for measuring the value of new knowledge are similarly hard and quantifiable – increased efficiency, lower costs, improved return on investment.

But there is another way to think about knowledge and its role in business organisations. It is found most commonly at highly successful Japanese competitors like Honda, Canon, Matsushita, NEC, Sharp, and Kao. These companies have become famous for their ability to respond quickly to customers, create new markets, rapidly develop new products, and dominate emergent technologies. The secret of their success is their unique approach to managing the creation of new knowledge.

To Western managers, the Japanese approach often seems odd or even incomprehensible. Consider the following examples:

- How is the slogan 'Theory of Automobile Evolution' a meaningful design concept for a new car? And yet, this phrase led to the creation of the Honda City, Honda's innovative urban car.
- Why is a beer can a useful analogy for a personal copier? Just such an analogy caused a fundamental breakthrough in the design of Canon's revolutionary mini-copier, a product that created the personal copier market and has led Canon's successful migration from its stagnating camera business to the more lucrative field of office automation.
- What possible concrete sense of direction can a made-up word such as 'optoelectronics' provide to a company's product-development engineers? Under this rubric, however, Sharp has developed a reputation for creating 'first products' that define new technologies and markets, making Sharp a major player in businesses ranging from colour televisions to liquid crystal displays to customised integrated circuits.

In each of these cases, cryptic slogans that to a Western manager sound just plain silly – appropriate for an advertising campaigns perhaps, but certainly not for running a company – are in fact highly effective tools for creating new knowledge. Managers everywhere recognise the serendipitous quality of innovation. Executives at these Japanese companies are *managing* that serendipity to the benefit of the company, its employees and its customers.

The centrepiece of the Japanese approach is the recognition that creating new knowledge is not simply a matter of 'processing' objective information. Rather, it depends on tapping the tacit and often highly subjective insights, intuitions, and hunches of individual employees and making those insights available for testing and use by the company as a whole. The key to this process is personal commitment, the employees' sense of identity with the enterprise and its mission. Mobilising that commitment and embodying tacit knowledge in actual technologies and products require managers who are as comfortable with images and symbols – slogans such as Theory of Automobile Evolution, analogies like that between a personal copier and a beer can, metaphors such as 'optoelectronics' – as they are with hard numbers measuring market share, productivity, or ROI.

The more holistic approach to knowledge at many Japanese companies is also founded on another fundamental insight. A company is not a machine but a living organism. Much like an individual, it can have a collective sense of identity and fundamental purpose. This is the organisational equivalent of self-knowledge – a shared understanding of what the company stands for, where it is going, what kind of world it wants to live in, and most important, how to make that world a reality.

The key lessons for managers is quite simple . . . any company that wants to compete on knowledge must also learn from Japanese techniques of knowledge creation.

In this respect, the knowledge-creating company is as much about ideals as it is about ideas. And that fact fuels innovation. The essence of innovation is to re-create the world according to a particular vision or ideal. To create

new knowledge means quite literally to re-create the company and everyone in it in a non-stop process of personal and organisational
self-renewal. In the knowledge-creating company, inventing new knowledge is not a specialised activity – the province of the R&D department or
marketing or strategic planning. It is a way of behaving, indeed a way of
being, in which everyone is a knowledge worker – that is to say, an entrepreneur.

The reasons why Japanese companies seem especially good at this kind
of continuous innovation and self-renewal are complicated. But the key
lesson for managers is quite simple: much as manufacturers around the
world have learned from Japanese manufacturing techniques, any company that wants to compete on knowledge must also learn from Japanese
techniques of knowledge creation . . .

Source: Reprinted by permission of *Harvard Business Review*. From Ikujiro Nonaka, 'The knowledge-creating company', *Harvard Business Review*, November–December, 1991, pp. 96–7. Copyright 1991 by the President and Fellows of Harvard College; all rights reserved.

Different companies and different countries will leverage knowledge,
their intangible asset, differently to restructure their organizations,
develop talent within their organizations, develop and maintain collaborative relationships with their competitors, cement their merger
relations, and bring about innovation in products and processes.

KNOWLEDGE AND TRANSFORMATION OF A NATIONAL ECONOMY – INDIA'S SOFTWARE INDUSTRY

Knowledge combined with technology can transform the economy of
a nation. Not long ago India was categorized as an underdeveloped
country and yet today Indian software is at work around the world.
What factors have brought such a transformation. The answer lies in
the knowledge workers.

According to the *Financial Times* (1995), top Indian software companies offer technical competence, lower costs and prompt delivery:

The emergence of India's software industry is a remarkable success story – in both domestic and international terms. Today, India is the preferred choice for many western companies for outsourcing their software development projects.

Highlighting this, the industry grew by more than 50 per cent last year posting total turnover of about $850 million, according to India's National Association of Software and Service Companies. Add to this, the value of in-house development of software and the figure rises to about $41 billion. Less than 10 years ago, the industry was worth a mere $10 million.

India's key competitive advantage is the sheer size, technical competence and relatively low cost of its manpower base. With more than 1.4 million software programmers, India has the second largest English-speaking scientific manpower pool after the US, and a sophisticated higher education system producing a steady stream of highly qualified graduates.

Knowledge combined with technology can transform the economy of a nation.

These advantages have helped India's software exports grow by 30 per cent a year in dollar terms to reach almost $500m last year (1994) and helped attract a string of foreign investments into the sector in the 1980s.

Today, a wide range of western companies – including Citicorp, Digital Equipment, Texas Instruments, Motorola, Siemens and Unisys – have Indian operations which serve as software engineering and production centres for their worldwide operations.

India's success story of the software industry shows clearly how knowledge can be leveraged to gain and sustain competitive advantage.

VERDICT

The key productive resources of the new era are neither land, labour nor capital but knowledge, core competencies and customers. These are the factors of production of the information age. Knowledge as a factor of production has to be taken very seriously by economists. According to Thomas Stewart, author of Intellectual Capital: The New Wealth of Organisations, *in the US the proportion of knowledge workers (those working with information rather than things) will have increased from 17 per cent to 59 per cent over the course of the twentieth century. In the year 1991 US business spent more money on information technology than on production plant and equipment.*

THE LEARNING ORGANIZATION

To be knowledge-based, it is essential for an organization to put itself in a learning mode. Learning organizations, according to Peter Senge (1990) are places 'where people continually expand their capacity to create results they truly desire, where new and expansive patterns of thinking are nurtured, where collective aspiration is set free, and where people are continually learning how to learn together.'

According to Senge, learning organizations need to have the following attributes:

- the concept of the learning organization is a vision;
- the learning organization is continually expanding its capacity to be creative and innovative;
- learning has to be intrinsically motivating;
- learning is about acquiring new knowledge and enhancing existing knowledge;

To be knowledge-based, it is essential for an organization to put itself in a learning mode

- learning has intellectual (thinking) and pragmatic (doing) dimensions;
- learning requires commitment and responsibility;
- learning is about developing core competencies;
- open and frank communication is one of the pre-requisites of learning;
- many organizations in practice have learning disabilities and some are very slow learners; the following are the reasons why this happens:
  - it is difficult to forget past habits – unlearning is far more difficult than learning;
  - there is a belief that 'if it ain't broke don't fix it';
  - there is cultural resistance;
  - it is unsettling to disturb the 'status quo';
  - people are unable to identify core competencies;
  - resources are lacking to update core competencies;
  - there is no commitment and conviction from the top.

To become a knowledge-based company and gain competitive advantage, it is important to eliminate causes of learning disabilities.

FROM COMPARATIVE ADVANTAGE TO COMPETITIVE ADVANTAGE

The concept of 'comparative advantage' is at the core of economics of international trade. Trade between countries takes place for a variety of reasons. The main reason was put forward by David Ricardo in the nineteenth century, which was that trade takes place because of differences in *comparative advantage*.

The law of comparative advantage states that countries specialize in producing and exporting those goods that they can produce at a lower relative cost than other countries. Costs differ due to differences in technology and/or productivity. The focus of attention is on the opportunity costs in relation to the factors of production used. These factors are land, labour and capital. The relative productivity differences form the basis of international trade. Countries specialize in producing the goods they make *relatively* cheaply.

The concept of comparative advantage has some merit but it is based on the productivity and cost differences of the traditional factors of production and it also depends on resource endowments. These factors have been transformed and now we need to consider core competencies, customers and knowledge at macro level to explain trade and production patterns. To do so we have to talk about competitive advantage as opposed to comparative advantage. There is no natural home for knowledge and competencies.

> *The choice of competitive scope, or the range of a firm's activities, plays a powerful role in determining competitive advantage.*

Competitive advantage, according to Professor Michael Porter, is at the heart of a firm's performance in competitive markets. How organizations at micro level use generic strategies incorporating cost leadership, differentiation and focus to position themselves in a competitive arena is what the modern business is all about and it is also how these organizations trade internationally. The choice of competitive scope, or the range of a firm's activities, plays a powerful role in determining competitive advantage.

According to Lester Throw, it is not the rules of the game that have changed but the game itself. Comparative advantage was a positive-sum game. Everybody had their own niche. The present game is a zero-sum game.

BACK TO GLOBALIZATION

This book started with the topic of globalization and how the globalization process has diffused the clear concepts of demand, supply and the markets. The process is reinforced with the changes taking place in technologies, in governments' policies in relation to liberalization of trade and political ideologies. Professor Vijay Govindarajan of Amos Tuck School of Business Administration, and Professor Anil Gupta (1999) of the University of Maryland highlight the extent of the changes taking place in the economic landscape:

> We live in an increasingly global world. What this means in practical terms is that if you are the chairman of Nucor Steel you consider Brazil as well as the US when deciding where to locate a new $700m mini-mill.
>
> If you are the chairman of Ford, you enter emerging markets such as China or India with modified versions of existing cars such as the Escort or Ka instead of designing a new car from scratch.
>
> If you are India's finance minister, you view the integration of India's economy with the rest of the world as fundamental to the country's transformation into an economic superpower.
>
> And if you are a junior manager at Proctor & Gamble, you have virtually no chance of making it into the top ranks of the company unless you combine superb on-the-job performance with extensive international experience.
>
> Such is life today in the global village. The economic landscape is not the same as it was 20 years ago, nor is the pace of global economic change expected to slacken in the next 20 years.

There is now a growing economic interdependence among countries in spite of the formation of various regional blocks. At macro level between 1989 and 1996, cross-border trade in goods and services grew at an average annual rate of 6.2 per cent – almost twice as fast as the average annual growth rate of 3.2 per cent in the world's GDP during the same period.

At micro level, joint ventures and sourcing are taking place across borders. Boeing is buying materials in China, fashion and clothing firms are manufacturing in the Asian Pacific countries, and there are numerous examples of manufacturing and service firms sourcing material in different countries. Global sourcing is influenced partly by comparative advantage but organizations now also source capabilities in different countries. Witness the sourcing of software skills and capabilities from India and Ireland by computer companies based in Silicon Valley.

The 1990s is also experiencing a significant amount of cross-border alliances and mergers. In the retailing sector, Carrefour has a 60:40 joint venture with President Enterprise in Taiwan; Ahold, a Dutch group, has a 50:50 joint venture with Venturtech Investment Corporation in China. In other sectors ABB's acquisition of Westinghouse's transmission and distribution operation, BA's proposed alliance with American Airlines, Boeing's acquisition of McDonnell Douglas, Corning's joint venture with Siemens to produce fibre-optic cable, the GM-Suzuki joint venture in Canada, the proposed merger of Chrysler and BMW are but some of the examples which reflect global partnerships and collaboration to win competitive advantage.

In *Business Week* (7 August 1995) was the story of Texas Instruments' high speed telecommunications chip which was conceived by engineers from Ericsson Telephone Co. in Sweden and designed in Nice with software tools the company developed in Houston. Today's TCM 9055 chip rolls off the production line in Japan and Dallas, gets tested in Taiwan and is wired into Ericsson line-cards that monitor phone systems in Sweden, the US, Mexico and Australia.

Instead of focusing attention on relative costs and productivity, modern businesses also consider safety, time to market, on-time delivery, quality, technology and price. They do this to gain and sustain competitive advantage.

Apart from global trends, other factors such as historical hang-ups, chance and government intervention in terms of subsidies also overturn the principle of comparative advantage.

According to Michael Porter (1990):

In a world of increasingly global competition, nations have become more, not less, important. As the basis of competition has shifted more and more to the creation of knowledge, the role of the nation has grown. Competitive advantage is created and sustained through a highly localised process. Differences in national values, culture, economic structures, institutions, and histories all contribute to competitive success. There are striking differences in the pattern of competitiveness in every country; no nation can or will be competitive in every or even most industries. Ultimately, nations succeed in particular industries because their home environment is the most forward-looking, dynamic, and challenging.

Source: Reprinted by permission of *Harvard Business Review*. From Michael E. Porter, 'The competitive advantage of nations', *Harvard Business Review*, March–April, 1990. Copyright 1990 by the President and Fellows of Harvard College; all rights reserved.

Finally, to quote Alvin Tofler:

While land, labour, raw materials and capital were the main factors of production in the Second Wave economy of the past, knowledge – broadly defined here to include data, information, images, symbols, culture, ideology and values – is now the central resource of the Third Wave economy.

VERDICT

At micro and macro level there has been fundamental change in the way business and trade are conducted. The traditional factors of production have been transformed significantly and they are replaced by new factors of production – competencies, knowledge and customers. These factors are very dynamic which make the concept of comparative advantage inappropriate in new economics. At micro as well as macro level, what matters is the gaining and sustaining of comparative advantage.

EXECUTIVE SUMMARY

- Knowledge is one of the key factors of production in the new economic scenario.

- As a factor of production, knowledge is an appreciating asset governed by increasing returns.

- Various writers are now advocating the use of knowledge management in organizations.

- 3M and Hewlett-Packard are presented as case studies of knowledge-driven companies.

- Professor Thomas Davenport presents ten principles of knowledge management.

- Japanese companies adopt a different perspective to knowledge management within their organizations.

- To be a knowledge-driven company, organizations have first to be learning organizations.

- Many organizations have learning disabilities. These have to be eliminated in order to gain competitive advantage.

- The concept of competitive advantage has overturned the principle of comparative advantage in traditional economics. In new economics competitive advantage, which is a dynamic concept, should be the main driver of trade.

References

Davenport, Thomas (1996) 'Some principles of knowledge management', *Strategy & Business*, Winter, 34–40.

Day, Jonathan D. and Wendler, James C. (1998) 'The new economics of organization', *The McKinsey Quarterly*, 1, 6–9.

Edvinson, Leif and Sullivan, Patrick (1996) 'Developing a model for managing intellectual capital', *European Management Journal*, 14, August, 357–8.

Financial Times (1995) 'Review of Information Technology' 6 December.

Govindarajan, Vijay and Gupta, Anil (1999) 'Setting a course for the new global landscape' in FT *Mastering Global Business*. London: Financial Times Management, 5–11.

Graham, Ann and Pizzo, Vincent (1996) 'A question of balance: strategic knowledge management', *European Management Journal*, 14, August, 338.

McKinsey Quarterly Editorial (1998) 'Best practice and beyond: knowledge strategies', *The McKinsey Quarterly*, 1, 19–25.

Nonaka, Ikujiro (1991) 'The knowledge-creating company', *Harvard Business Review*, November–December, 96–7.

Porter, Michael (1990) 'The competitive advantage of nations', *Harvard Business Review*, March–April.

Senge, Peter (1990) *The Fifth Disciple – the Art and Practice of the Learning Organisation*, USA: Century Business.

CONCLUSION –
LET'S BITE THE BULLET

Economists have to be conversant with what is happening not just at macroeconomic level but also at microeconomic level. Dramatic changes are taking place in the business world and developments in technology are accelerating these changes. The discipline of economics has to lead rather than lag behind these changes.

However hard and uncomfortable it might be, economists have to review and revise the discipline of economics and make it more meaningful to the business world. They have to transform it from 'dismal science' to 'useful science' not only providing insights into what is happening now but preparing the business world for the things to come. It is, therefore, time to bite the bullet and push economics to enter the information age thus bringing about the fusion of economics with business.

SUGGESTED READING FOR
KNOWLEDGE WORKERS

Crainer, S. (1988) *Key Management Ideas*. London: Financial Times Management.

Begg, David; Fischer, Stanley and Dormbusch, Rudiger, (1994) *Economics*. UK: McGraw Hill.

Drucker, Peter (1989) *The New Realities*. Oxford, England: Butterworth-Heinemann.

FT Mastering Management (1997), London: Financial Times Management.

FT Mastering Global Business (1999), London: Financial Times Management.

'Global strategies: insights from the world's leading thinkers', *Harvard Business Review* (1984), Harvard Business School Press.

Kermally, S. (1996) *Total Management Thinking*. Oxford, England: Butterworth-Heinemann.

Koch, R. and Campbell, A. (1993) *Wake Up & Shake Up Your Company*, London: Financial Times Management.

Kotler, P. (1994) *Marketing Management*. USA: Prentice Hall

Naisbitt, J. and Aburdene P. (1990) *Megatrends 2000*. London: Sidgwick & Jackson.

Samuelson, Paul A. and Nordhaus, William D. (1995) *Economics*. USA: McGraw Hill.

Peters, Tom (1997) *The Circle of Innovation*. USA: Alfred A. Knopp.

Senge, P.M (1990) *The Fifth Discipline*. USA: Century Business.

Tichy, N.M. and Sherman, S. (1993) *Control Your Destiny or Someone Else Will*. USA: Harper Business.

INDEX